Hodder
Children's
Books
a division of Hodder Headline Limited

Text copyright © Bob Fowke, illustrations copyright © Andrew Mee 2002

The right of Bob Fowke to be identified as the author of the work has been asserted by him in accordance with the Copyright, Designs and Patents Act 1988.

Produced by Fowke & Co. for Hodder Children's Books

Cover picture: supplied by the Museum of London. From Guy Fawkes volume, image number 6822.

Published by Hodder Children's Books 2002

0 340 85182 1

10 9 8 7 6 5 4 3 2 1

Hodder Children's Books
a division of Hodder Headline Limited
338 Euston Road
London NW1 3BH

Printed and bound by the Guernsey Press Co. Ltd., Channel Islands
A Catalogue record for this book is available from the British Library

CONTENTS

 Watch out for the *Sign of the Foot*! Whenever you see this sign in the book it means there are some more details at the *FOOT* of the page. Like here.

GOT A MATCH?

THINKING UP A PLOT

I. HOW IT WAS MEANT TO BE

...A TRAIL OF SLOW—BURNING POWDER — THAT SHOULD DO NICELY FOR A FUSE...

...LIGHT THE FUSE...

...LEAVE ENOUGH TIME FOR A GETAWAY...

...THEN...

BOOM!!

HA!

KING JAMES 1

...THAT'LL PUT PAID TO THE KING AND HIS PARLIAMENT!..

LORD SALISBURY

CHARLES, PRINCE OF WALES

LORDS

MEMBERS OF PARLIAMENT

2. How it wasn't meant to be

A TRAIL OF SLOW-BURNING POWDER – THAT SHOULD DO NICELY FOR A FUSE...

BUT WHAT'S THAT NOISE?..

GOTCHA!!

THE NAME'S JOHNSON, SIR, JOHN JOHNSON!

GUY FAWKES, ACTUALLY!

THEY'VE CAUGHT GUY FAWKES!

OH NO!

RUN FOR IT!

FLEE!

TO THE HORSES!

LET'S GO!

The right season for treason

The 'Gunpowder Plot' as we call it today, or 'Powder Treason' as it was then known, was a plot by fanatical

Treason is serious disloyalty to a ruler, whether king or parliament.

English Roman Catholics to blow up the House of Lords on 5 November 1605, murdering around three hundred people in the process. Most English Catholics would have been horrified by the idea. Guy Fawkes's job was to light the fuse which would set off a massive explosion of thirty-six barrels of gunpowder. The plotters chose 5 November for their dreadful deed, because that was the date set by King James I for the grand opening of a new parliament. On that day members of both the houses of Lords and Commons, together with the king and his son, would be gathered in the House of Lords for the opening ceremony. One big explosion would have polished off the lot of them.

Fortunately for King and Parliament, the plot was uncovered by Robert Cecil, James's leading statesman. All the plotters were caught - or died resisting arrest.

AND THE REASON FOR TREASON

English Roman Catholics were fed up because King James, who was not a Roman Catholic, refused to allow them to practise their religion freely. At that time, Catholics were punished if they held Roman Catholic church services, even in the privacy of their own homes. If they were caught, Roman Catholic priests might be executed. Even though they were fed up, most English Roman Catholics were prepared to put up with this state of affairs because they knew that things would get even worse for them if they resisted. But some young hot-heads felt that they had to fight back, come what may. It was these young (and not-so-young) hot-heads who planned the Gunpowder Plot. They meant it to be the start of a massive 'stir' of Roman Catholics throughout the country.

As things turned out, when it was over Roman Catholics were far worse off after the Plot than they'd been before. And from that time on, by special act of Parliament, 5 November has been a day of national celebration. From that day to this, on 5 November - Bonfire Night - the whole country celebrates Parliament's lucky escape.

And poor old Guy Fawkes gets burned - over and over and over again.

 Stir was a common word for an uprising at that date.

I HATE YOU!!

GRR!!

RELIGION FOR PIGEONS
MAGIC!

In the early seventeenth century, people believed in many things which they no longer believe in today. They believed that the visible world around them was just part of an invisible world of angels and devils, of witches and magic. Religion, the most important part of *both* worlds, was deadly serious. Many, if not most, people started and ended each day with prayers with lots of other little prayers in between, such as grace before and after meals. God was real and the devil was real too - as were the flames of hell. If you believed in the wrong things, hell was where you ended up.

WELCOME TO THE NETHERMOST PIT OF HELL! YOU ARE HERE BECAUSE YOU DIDN'T BELIEVE IN GOD - OR ME !!

ER... I'M WILLING TO RECONSIDER...

Magic too was real, and the dividing line between religion and magic was very thin. After all, even nowadays, if you kneel down and ask God for a new bike, are you praying - or casting a spell? James wrote

9

a serious book about magic: *Daemonology*, all about witchcraft and devil-worship.

 **WITCHES' BREW**

To understand why people took their religion so seriously it helps to understand some of the other things they believed in as well:

In Europe as a whole, over 100,000 people were burned as witches between 1500 and 1700.

BUT I'M NOT A WITCH!

THAT'S BECAUSE I'M BURNING, YOU FOOL!

BAH! YOU SMELL LIKE A WITCH! ALL SMOKY, LIKE THE DEVIL!

CAN YOU DO IT?

YES - I'VE GOT JUST THE SPELL FOR IT!

ye evil Spelles

SILLY YOUNG FOOL - MORE MONEY THAN SENSE!

Even among the upper classes, it was widely believed that spells worked. For instance, a Mrs Anne Turner cast spells to help a Lady Frances Howard get rid of her unwanted husband so that she could marry Robert Kerr, a close friend of James I 👣.

An Act of Parliament of 1603 allowed the death penalty for those making spells, an activity described as 'conference with the devil'.

I'VE GOT SOME GREAT IDEAS FOR A SPOT OF EVIL!

GOOD - GOOD! TELL ME MORE!

 Anne Turner was also said to have helped in the poisoning of Sir Thomas Overbury, a former friend of Robert Kerr.

I PROTEST!

Given that religion was so important, it's hardly surprising that disagreements about religion led to arguments. The big argument, that between *Catholics* and a group of break-away Christians called *Protestants*, had been going on for nearly a hundred years before James I became King of England:

Once upon a time, all the Christians in western Europe, which meant almost all Europeans, belonged to the Roman Catholic church. The Pope in Rome was their religious leader.

In the early sixteenth century, some Christians, soon to be called 'Protestants', led by the German priest, Martin Luther, broke away from the Catholic church to form separate churches. This was because they disagreed with various Roman Catholic beliefs and because they thought that the Catholic church had become corrupt.

11

On top of that, the break-away Christians were fed up with sending lots of money to support the Pope in Rome. The Pope lived very luxuriously.

The people who followed Martin Luther and broke away from the main church were called 'Protestants' because they 'protested' about the things they disliked.

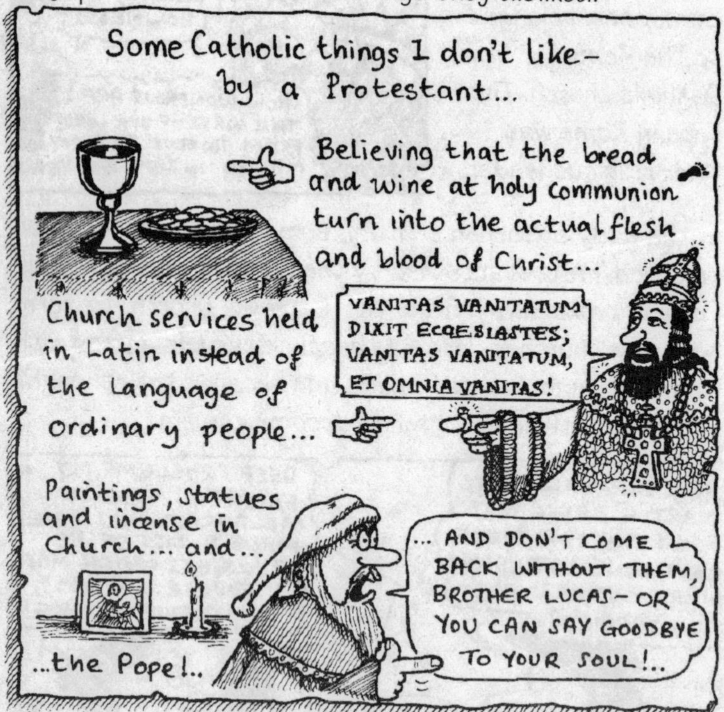

Some Catholic things I don't like — by a Protestant...

Believing that the bread and wine at holy communion turn into the actual flesh and blood of Christ...

Church services held in Latin instead of the language of ordinary people...

VANITAS VANITATUM DIXIT ECCLESIASTES; VANITAS VANITATUM, ET OMNIA VANITAS!

Paintings, statues and incense in Church... and...

...the Pope!..

...AND DON'T COME BACK WITHOUT THEM, BROTHER LUCAS — OR YOU CAN SAY GOODBYE TO YOUR SOUL!..

At Holy Communion special bread and wine are handed out to the congregation by the priest, in memory of the last supper of Jesus before he died on the cross.

THE MARK OF THE BEAST
- BUT WHOSE BEAST?

Catholics never accepted the new, break-away, Protestant version of Christianity. For them, almost by definition, there was only one church - their church. Protestants were heretics , in fact they weren't really Christians at all and, according to the Catholics, it was impossible for a Protestant to pray to God. If a man was ordained as a vicar in the (Protestant) Church of England, they said that he'd received 'the mark of the beast', meaning the devil. In countries where Catholics were in control, if they caught a Protestant they often burned him or her at the stake.

For their part, Protestants barely accepted that Catholics were Christians either. They thought that Catholicism was silly and an insult to God. They didn't usually burn Catholics, but they could be almost equally nasty.

A *heretic* is someone who disagrees with the official teachings of the Church.

Ordination is the ceremonial appointment of a Christian priest.

13

EEK! C. OF EEEK!

England broke away from the Roman Catholic Church in 1534, when the Tudor King, Henry VIII, wanted to divorce his first wife and the Pope wouldn't let him. From that time on, England became increasingly Protestant. Not that the Church of England ever became ultra-Protestant. Like so many English things, it was safely middle-of-the-road. In the early days, all but extreme Catholics felt that they could belong to it. It even had bishops, just as Catholics did:

INTENSIVE VICAR FARM

These sixteenth-century, Church of England vicars are being intensively farmed so that a new crop will be ready to guide the church through the coming century, but some things are wrong. What are they?

COME ON YOU LOT! CREDO TIME!

YEAH! HURRY UP!

HEY! NOLI ME TANGERE!

At the first ... the greatest part even of those who in their judgements and affections had before bin Catholickes, did not well discern any great fault, novelty or difference from the former religion ...

There were a few differences however: church services were held in English not Latin, and it was believed that the bread and wine at Holy Communion stayed just that - bread and wine. This may seem like a minor point nowadays, but it was very important in those days.

Answer
What's wrong is that some of the vicars are speaking Latin. A few other minor details are wrong as well - see page 122.

PURITANS

However, some Church-of-England Protestants were more extreme than others. The extremists disapproved of anything which smacked of Catholicism, or 'Popery' as they called it. They disapproved of statues in churches, bishops, incense and religious painting, and they believed that only the 'elect' chosen by God would enter heaven and 'reprobates', meaning everyone else, were damned. 'Puritan' was a term of abuse for all such extreme Protestants. They often gave their children odd names such as 'Sorry-for-sin' or 'Fly-Fornication'.

By the early 1600s, Puritanism was becoming more popular. This was dangerous because most Puritans really hated Catholicism. Evidence of growing hatred could be found in night-time attacks on Catholic statues and pictures. The cross in West Cheap in London which was decorated with a statue of Jesus's mother, the Virgin Mary, was a favourite target:

... the image of our Lady was again defaced, by plucking off her crown and almost her head and stabbing her in the breast ...

GOT THE PLOT?

A TROT THROUGH THE PLOTS
CONTRARY MARY

As soon as Protestantism reared its head, the major Catholic powers of Europe, Spain in particular, tried to stamp it out. Europe was torn apart by terrifying religious wars. England avoided the worst of the fighting, but nowhere was safe.

Spain, then a European super-power, tried to force Protestant countries back into the Catholic fold. Spanish armies battered the Protestants in the Low Countries, still officially part of the Spanish Empire. In France the French king hammered French Protestants.

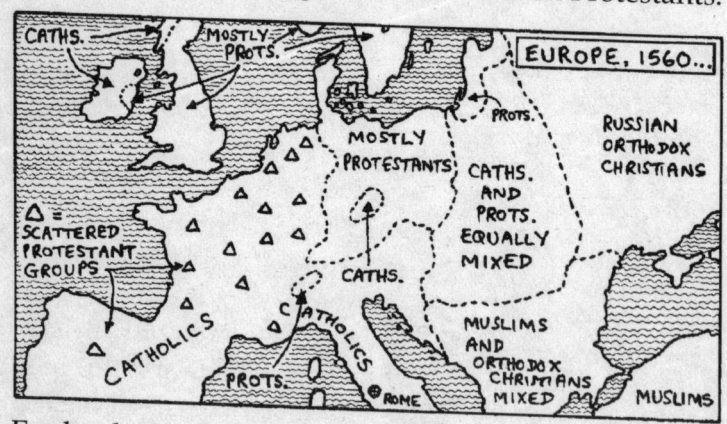

England was by far the strongest of the Protestant countries. Money and arms from England fuelled Protestant armies fighting Spain on the continent. If England could be 'won' back to Catholicism then the way would be clear for total Catholic victory in Europe. Spanish kings saw it as their religious duty to try to help a Catholic monarch onto the throne of England. This happened in 1553, when Mary Tudor became Queen of England. 'Bloody Mary' as she became known was a very keen Catholic. She married Philip II of Spain in 1554 and tried to force England back into being a Catholic country. Three hundred English Protestants, including bishops, were burned to death in the process.

THESE SO-CALLED PROTESTANTS ARE JUST HERETICS, REALLY! SO NOW WE'RE CATHOLIC AGAIN WE'LL HAVE TO BURN THEM! I MUST MAKE A LIST!... ROGERS, HOOPER, RIDLEY, LATIMER, CRANMER —DEFINITELY CRANMER!...

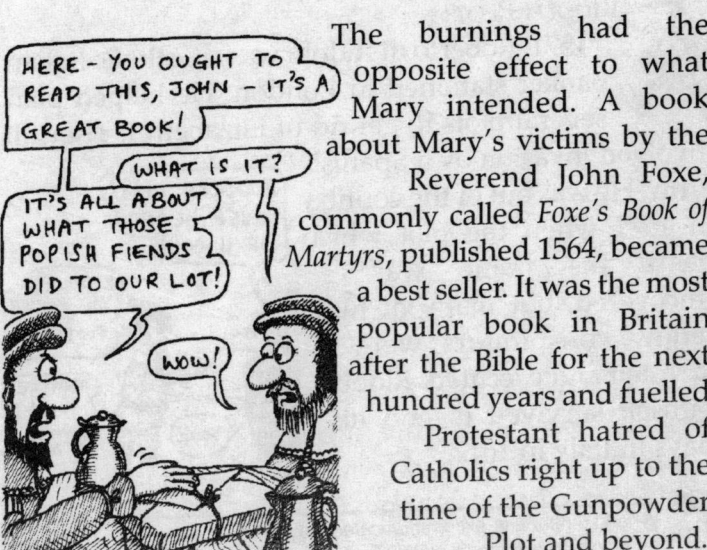

HERE - YOU OUGHT TO READ THIS, JOHN - IT'S A GREAT BOOK!

WHAT IS IT?

IT'S ALL ABOUT WHAT THOSE POPISH FIENDS DID TO OUR LOT!

WOW!

The burnings had the opposite effect to what Mary intended. A book about Mary's victims by the Reverend John Foxe, commonly called *Foxe's Book of Martyrs*, published 1564, became a best seller. It was the most popular book in Britain after the Bible for the next hundred years and fuelled Protestant hatred of Catholics right up to the time of the Gunpowder Plot and beyond.

LOSING THE PLOT
I. DISHING LIZ

Mary died in 1558 and her sister, the Protestant Elizabeth I, became queen. Then, in 1570, the Pope excommunicated  Elizabeth and told English Catholics that they didn't have to obey her. In other words, he told English Catholics to become traitors. This *really* fuelled Protestant fear of Catholics.

At the same time as the Pope was advising English Catholics to turn traitor, Spanish monarchs poured money into plots to get rid of Elizabeth ...

RIDOLFI PLOT

1571: Roberto di Ridolfi was a Catholic Italian banker stationed in London. He helped plan several plots to get rid of Elizabeth I. They all involved invasion by a Spanish army. He was out of the country in 1571 when the plot which bears his name was uncovered, but many of his fellow conspirators were arrested and executed. Ridolfi himself survived to end his days in Italy in 1612.

 When someone is *excommunicated* they are cast out of the Church and no longer allowed to take Holy Communion and other such 'sacraments'.

THROCKMORTON PLOT

1583: Francis Throckmorton, an English Catholic, was executed in 1583, for plotting to kill Elizabeth I. His plot was for a Spanish army to invade England backed by a general uprising of Catholics. Elizabeth would be killed and her Catholic cousin, Mary Queen of Scots, would rule in her place.

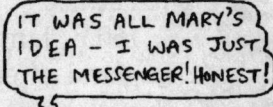

BABINGTON PLOT

1586: Anthony Babington, an English Catholic, plotted with fellow Catholics to release Mary Queen of Scots from prison in the north of England where she was being held by Elizabeth. Elizabeth's agents uncovered letters from the plotters to Mary in her prison, hidden in waterproof leather packets in beer barrels. As with the Throckmorton Plot, the plan was for Elizabeth to be killed and for Mary to take her place on the throne. Babington was executed in 1586. Mary Queen of Scots had her own head chopped off the following year.

Losing the plot

2. Junking James

Bye Plot

1603: James I, a Protestant, governed England after Elizabeth's death in 1603. The Bye plot was a Catholic plan to kidnap James and keep him prisoner in the Tower of London until he granted the demands of Catholics. It was a mad scheme and it was led by a mad Catholic priest called Father Watson. Watson had expected James to grant immediate religious toleration to Catholics as soon as he arrived in England and was disappointed when James didn't. Watson's plot became known as the 'Treason of the Bye' to distinguish it from another plot of about the same time, the 'Treason of the Main'. Both plots were uncovered in July 1603.

WHAT A DAFT PLOT! WATSON, YOU'RE BARMY!

I AM NOT BARMY! FTANG!

EEK!

FTANG!!

Main Plot

1603: The Main Plot was more serious than the Bye Plot. James 'and his cubs' were to be killed and James's cousin, Lady Arbella Stuart, was to be put on the throne to rule in his place. More serious but just as mad: Lady Arbella was a dyed-in-the-wool Protestant and would never have agreed to the plan even if she'd known about it. James, who was a very merciful king for his time, decided not to execute several leading noblemen who were involved in it.

HMM! WE DON'T WANT ANY MORE MARTYRS!...

THEY'VE GOT TOO MANY RELATIVES!

A BIT OF PADDING

James I's coronation as King of England took place on 15 March 1604. So the Bye and Main plots were uncovered *before* he was crowned and when he'd only just arrived in the country from Scotland, hardly a friendly way for Catholics to greet their new monarch - especially a monarch who was terrified of being murdered. James I always wore specially padded clothes as protection against stabbing.

BY HEAVENS! IS IT ALWAYS SO HOT IN LONDON?

PERHAPS SIRE IS A LITTLE OVERDRESSED?..

HAH! I COULD DO BETTER THAN THAT!

JAMES VISITS THE THAMES

NEW KING PROMISES GOOD TIMES FOR ALL

LET'S START WITH A BANG

James I was a Scotsman and spoke with a strong Scots accent. When he arrived in England in 1603, he'd already been king of Scotland for thirty-six years. The Gunpowder Plotters had *two* reasons to want to blow him up:

HE'S A PROT!

AND A STINKER!

YUK!

1. He was a Protestant.
2. He was Scottish.

James had been crowned James VI of Scotland in 1567, when he was just thirteen months old, in place of his mother, Catholic Mary Queen of Scots, whom we've just heard about. In the short time before he was crowned, enough had happened to James to justify his fear of murder. His father, tall, handsome, drunk Lord Darnley, murdered his mother's favourite and secretary, the Italian David Rizzio. Next year (1567), Darnley himself was strangled, and the house where he was staying in Edinburgh was destroyed in a massive explosion.

BOOM!

Most people thought that Mary Queen of Scots was behind the murder. Mary was imprisoned by the leading (Protestant) Scottish lords but escaped and fled to England, where she was locked up by Elizabeth I, as we've already seen.

A PROT SCOT

James grew up Protestant because he was left behind in Scotland in the care of his mother's Protestant enemies. He never knew his mother and couldn't remember what she looked like. In later life he tried hard not to believe that she was the murderess of his father, although he didn't love her.

The woman who really mattered to him was Queen Elizabeth I of England, she who executed his mother. Elizabeth had the power to name him as her heir, and England was to Scotland as a big, juicy grapefruit is to a shrivelled prune - England was rich and Scotland was very poor.

From the moment that he began to rule independently, in June 1583 when he was just seventeen, James set out to become King of England as well as King of Scotland. To do this, he needed Elizabeth's help - which was a long drawn out business. James and Elizabeth wrote to each other often, but Elizabeth was hopeless at making up her mind about anything. In fact, she never actually named James as her heir. The most she managed was a nod of her head when asked if he should succeed her - and even *that* was when she was on her death bed.

BUT NOT AS PROT A SCOT AS ALL THAT

As well as keeping in with Elizabeth, James also had to reassure the King of Spain that he wasn't a threat to Catholics. Otherwise Spain might seize the moment of Elizabeth's death to carry out its old plan and put a Catholic monarch on England's throne. The death of a ruler was always a dangerous moment.

It helped that James's mother was Mary Queen of Scots. Mary became a Catholic heroine, almost a saint, after she was executed by Elizabeth. Catholics believed that some of the mother's 'virtues' must have passed to her son: they believed that the son of blessed Mary Queen of Scots was bound to be tolerant towards Catholics. James encouraged this idea. He was tolerant by nature anyway. His motto was *Beatti Pacifici*, 'Blessed are the Peacemakers'. He once told Elizabeth's chief minister, Robert Cecil:

I will never allow in my conscience that the blood of any man shall be shed for diversity of opinions in religion.

James changed his mind later, after bitter experience, but at that time he encouraged the idea that he might one day convert to Catholicism. It helped that in 1601 his beautiful young wife, Anne of Denmark, actually did convert . In 1602 the Pope himself backed James to be the next ruler of England. Nothing now stood in James's way.

LIZ DOES THE BIZ

Elizabeth I died early on 24 March 1603 and by 10 o'clock on the same morning, James had been proclaimed King of England. By 4 April he was on the road south to claim his new kingdom.

Being tolerant, James didn't object so long as she kept quiet about it. Anne probably converted to Catholicism because she couldn't stand the serious, Puritan Scottish lords who made the Scottish court a dull place. She reconverted late in life and died a Protestant.

All of England, Catholics as well as Protestants, rejoiced that an experienced ruler was ready to start ruling so quickly. Catholics were overjoyed. Elizabeth had treated them harshly and they expected better of James - as he'd led them to believe. They lost no time. When he reached York on 17 April, James was given a petition by a rather seedy gentleman, actually a Catholic priest in disguise called Father Hill. The petition asked that all the anti-Catholic laws in England be cancelled. However, James wasn't *that* tolerant. Father Hill was discovered to be a priest and thrown into prison. But it could have been worse - he could have been executed.

GLASS HOUSES

James loved his new kingdom. It was so *rich*. As he moved slowly south, he stayed in the houses of English noblemen. He could hardly believe his eyes. Several of them had more money than all his Scottish lords put together. Life was so much more *comfortable* than in Scotland. The Tudor nobles had turned their castles into stately homes with lots of windows and chimneys - still quite a new invention.

There was a rhyme about the great Tudor house Hardwick Hall in Derbyshire:

Hardwick hall
More glass than wall.

And the English were pleased to see him! This was amazing, considering that James was Scottish and therefore a foreigner and was surrounded by a band of Scottish cronies. The English looked down on foreigners. An Italian visitor described how, if they saw a handsome foreigner, the nicest thing they could think to say about him was:

He looks like an Englishman!

Not that the English, both Catholics and Protestants, *really* forgot their dislike of foreigners - including Scotsmen, who were thought to be 'stinking'. Crooks called 'swaggerers' began to prey on homeless Scots who followed James into England. When Guy Fawkes, the future plotter, visited Spain in July 1603, he let his anti-Scottish feelings show:

There is a natural hostility between the English and the Scots. There has always been one, and at present it keeps increasing.

29

SHUT OUTS

James was impressed by the riches of the English upper classes. The mass of the people were less comfortable but probably he hardly noticed them. Most people still lived in the country in one-room cottages. If they could afford it, they added extra rooms, called 'outshuts'.

Although desperately poor by modern standards, the people ate well compared to other countries. Slightly earlier, a Spaniard wrote home:

> *These English have their houses made of sticks and dirt, but fare commonly so well as the king.*

Poorest of the poor were the vagabonds. Vagabonds had no home village to fall back on when times were hard and they may have made up as much as ten per cent of the total population. Many of them had lost their land to sheep farming. Large open fields and common lands were being 'enclosed' (hedged or fenced in), by farmers and others, for sheep grazing.

I'LL HAE TAE GAE TAE ENGLAND FOR TAE LUIK FOR WORK, WIFIE — MAYBE THE SASSENACHS WILL BE A BRAW BIT KINDER THAN OOR AIN LAIRD!

I SHOULDN'T BANK ON IT, ANGUS!

AW, DA'!

LONDON

James and his cronies and all manner of other hangers-on, all hoping to profit from his new reign, arrived in London on 7 May. England was rich, but London was *loaded*. Describing the Strand a hundred years earlier (and the city had grown since then), an Italian reported:

> *There are fifty-two goldsmiths shops, so rich and full of silver vessels great and small, that in all the shops in Milan, Venice and Florence put together, I do not think there would be found so many of the magnificence.*

As for the people, the Duke of Wurtemberg described in 1592 how:

> *The inhabitants are magnificently apparelled and are extremely proud and overbearing ... they care little for foreigners, but scoff and laugh at them ...*

Luckily for James, the inhabitants, like the rest of the English, were pleased to see him. The Lord Mayor welcomed him in person as did large, friendly crowds. Although James never cared much for the attention of crowds. He once declared of an attentive crowd:

God's wounds! I will pull down my breeches and they shall also see my arse!

However, on this occasion he tried to be pleasant.

A GOOD START

James settled into the palace of Whitehall and started to rule as he intended to continue - tolerantly. Within a week, a Catholic priest, Father Weston, was released from the Tower of London. Since James's wife was a Catholic, James even allowed Catholic priests to visit his court, provided they pretended to be something else - keepers of the royal hawks or something.

And the best was yet to come.

A BETTER START

The *Act of Uniformity*, first passed by Parliament in 1549, was *not* an act which forced the people of England to wear uniforms ...

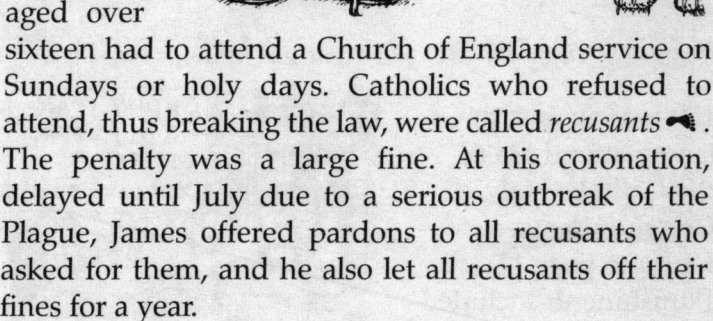

No, the Act of Uniformity said that everyone aged over sixteen had to attend a Church of England service on Sundays or holy days. Catholics who refused to attend, thus breaking the law, were called *recusants* . The penalty was a large fine. At his coronation, delayed until July due to a serious outbreak of the Plague, James offered pardons to all recusants who asked for them, and he also let all recusants off their fines for a year.

So far, so good. A letter writer of the period, John Chamberlain, remarked:

> *These bountiful beginnings put them in great hopes, insomuch that not only Protestants, but Papists* 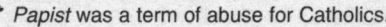 *and Puritans ... promise themselves great part in his (the King's) favour.'*

Recusant comes from the Latin *recusare*, to refuse.

Papist was a term of abuse for Catholics.

HIDEY HOLES AND SECRET CODES

SECRET PRIESTS IN SECRET PLACES

REASONS NOT TO BE CATHOLIC

When James became king of England in 1603, around 130,000 of his new subjects were Catholics (it's impossible to know the exact figure). Life had been tough on these people for years. If they wanted to practise their religion they had had to put up with the consequences. In the words of an old saying:

If you will enjoy the fire, you must put up with the smoke.

1. It was against the law to attend Mass, the Catholic Holy Communion (see footnote page 12). Punishments included a heavy fine or jail.

2. It was against the law to bring 'vain Popish trish trash' such as rosaries and crucifixes into the country. Punishments included life imprisonment.

Rosaries are prayer beads.
Crucifixes are statues of Christ on the Cross.

3. The heavy fines which recusants had to pay once a year were enough to bankrupt some of them. To avoid this, as many as 100,000 Catholics were 'church papists' - Catholics who went to Church of England services but went to Catholic mass in secret.

4. If Catholic priests were caught, they might be tortured, jailed or executed.

5. Convicted Catholics were forbidden to travel more than five miles from their homes.

RATLICS

You might imagine from the way they were treated, that Catholics were a different species, rats or something, to be got rid of. And that's how many people saw them. A pamphlet written in 1583, but not acted on, actually suggested that all Catholic children should be removed from their parents at the age of seven.

However, apart from being Catholics, in every other way these people were normal English men and women. Among them were many families of 'gentry'. Gentry were almost noblemen but not quite. They were the class of people who lived in the big hall in most villages and ran things locally. This meant that it was quite common for a Catholic family to own the local Church of England church and to appoint the local vicar. They might not *go* to the church but their Protestant servants would. Catholics were forbidden to have Catholic servants.

The Catholic gentry formed a secret network. They hid visiting priests in their large houses and allowed them to conduct secret services. Many of the priests were themselves English gentlemen and lived in disguise as 'friends' of wealthy Catholic families for years.

Douai see a Catholic?

Given what they'd had to endure in the previous fifty years, it's hardly surprising that English Catholics were a rare breed. As a breed, they had been saved from extinction by the *Catholic Mission*.

Back in 1568 a group of English Catholics founded an 'English College' at the new University of Douai, in what is now part of modern France. To the irritation of the locals, many young, Catholic Englishmen flocked to Douai to be trained as Catholic priests. Once trained and ordained (see footnote on page 13) their job was to

smuggle themselves back into England and to convert the English back to the 'true', Catholic religion. Since this was a crime, punishable by death, they had to be very brave young men.

A lonely shore

The first missionary priests landed in England in 1574. By 1600, three hundred of them had made the crossing. Not many survived: some were imprisoned, some were sent back abroad and some were executed.

Young Alexander Rawlins landed at night on a beach near Whitby in Yorkshire.

He was sheltered in the lonely farmhouse of a local fellow Catholic, a man called Thomas Warcop.

Rawlins' 'circuit' was a wide stretch of moorland and his 'flock' were the scattered Catholic families who still lived there.

Rawlins and Warcop were arrested during a search while hiding in Warcop's loft. Rawlins had his tell-tale Mass kit with him.

Rawlins was taken to York castle and questioned for hours while being made to kneel on one knee.

He was executed.

 The Mass kit would have contained sacred bread and wine, a crucifix and other such items.

IN SEARCH OF SAFETY

Catholic priests and their protectors lived in constant fear of arrest. If the authorities suspected that a priest was visiting a Catholic house, they would send 'poursuivants' to hunt him out. The poursuivants might arrive at any time. They would search high and low, tapping the walls to listen for the hollow sound of a secret chamber, lighting fires in the chimneys to smoke out hidden priests, even turfing people out of bed so that they could search the bedding. Searches might go on for days.

Special 'priestholes' were built where priests could hide until a search was over. The best of them were built by Nicholas Owen, known as 'Little John', the son of an Oxford carpenter. He was a tiny man with a limp caused by a packhorse falling on him. His small size made it easier for him to work in cramped spaces, for instance within the thick walls of old buildings. Owen always worked at night so that no one knew his secrets unless he told them.

LITTLE JOHN SPOT - OR, *SPOT LITTLE JOHN*

Some of Owen's secret chambers have never been discovered to this day.

THERE ARE FIVE PRIESTS HIDING IN THIS CUTAWAY HOUSE. CAN YOU FOLLOW THE SECRET PASSAGES AND FIND THEM?..

EMPTY

FALSE PRIESTHOLE (MEANT TO BE FOUND TO PUT SEARCHERS OFF THE SCENT)— WITH REAL ONE BEHIND

PRIESTHOLE IN A DRAIN

POO!

PRIESTS MIGHT HIDE IN ROOF SPACES

PRIESTHOLE IN A CHIMNEY— MIGHT GET A BIT HOT!

PRIESTHOLE IN THE THICKNESS OF AN OLD WALL

DURING LONG STAYS, A PRIEST MAY BE FED THROUGH A TUBE

SOUP!

EMPTY HOLE

41

A FINE THING

It was safer for a woman to break the anti-Catholic laws than for a man, because at that date most women, except widows, couldn't own property - so they couldn't pay fines!

Anne Vaux was a wealthy woman who rented several houses and converted them into safe houses for priests. Her house at Baddesley Clinton in Warwickshire could hide over twelve men in a number of secret chambers, some of them at the level of the moat.

THE TIDE TURNS

After James lifted the fines on recusants in 1603, many Catholics believed that the days of night searches and dark, clammy priestholes were coming to an end.

It is hardly credible in what jollity they now live.

Their husbands *could* be made to pay their fines for them, but that was thought to be a bit unfair on the husbands. It didn't happen very often.

42

Feeling safer, secret Catholics or 'Church papists' started to practise their faith more openly. Unfortunately, this made it seem to Protestants that Catholics were growing in number - that they were taking advantage of James's tolerance to create new converts. In reality, it just *seemed* like that because the Catholics had been hidden for so long. But anger against Catholics grew. It soon became obvious to James that his Protestant subjects were a lot less tolerant than he was, in fact dangerously so. On 19 March 1604, in a speech to the first Parliament of his reign, James seemed to plead for Protestants to compromise with the Catholics:

I would for my own part be content to meet them in the midway, so that all novelties might be renounced on either side.

But by then it was already too late. To reassure his Protestant subjects, James had spoken earlier of his:

... utter detestation (of Catholicism) ...

And just to show that he meant it, on 1 March all Catholic priests had been ordered to leave the country and the fines on recusants had been started up again - no wonder his pleas for compromise sounded pretty thin to Catholic ears. Then on 24 April, a bill in Parliament proposed that all Catholics should be classed as outlaws.

The bad old days were back.

ROTTER PLOTTERS

THE GUNPOWDER PLOT IS HATCHED

A HAIRY MOLE IS A GOOD MOLE

While the Catholics returned to square one, James moved on to square two: he settled down to enjoy himself. The Jacobean court was luxurious and corrupt, so corrupt that most senior statesmen took bribes from the Spanish government. Not that it helped the Spanish very much: bribery was a way of life. As the saying went:

Money is like muck, not good unless it be spread.

YOUR PARLIAMENT SPEECH, MY LORD...

AND A LITTLE GIFT FROM A FRIEND!

"1 MOST STRONGLY COMMEND THAT A NEW DOCK FOR SPANISH TRADE BE BUILT..." MM! LOOKS ALL RIGHT!

James allowed Catholics at court as company for his wife Anne, if she wanted them, but Anne didn't really bother about being a Catholic after she came to England. There were too many other things for her to enjoy. Among them, Jacobean fashions were exciting ...

Jacobean means 'of the time of King James'.

Face patches were just coming into fashion - if you didn't have any warts, which were thought to be lucky, especially if they were hairy warts. Also, Anne liked to wear the farthingale, a sort of shelf or padded bolster which held the skirt away from the hips. Fashionable women soon copied her. James, who was more serious than his wife, thought that farthingales took up too much room, which they did. He forbade anyone (man or woman!) to appear at court in:

1605: FACE-PATCHES WERE BLACK SILK OR MAKE-UP MOLES OR WARTS. LATER FACE-PATCHES COULD BE STARS, MOONS, DIAMONDS, etc:

FANCY LACE RUFF

FACE PATCH

TIARA

PEARL NECKLACE

LOW-CUT BODICE

JEWELLED FAN

WASP-WAIST CORSET

'WHEEL' FARTHINGALE HOLDS OUT SKIRT

LACE HANDKERCHIEF

FINELY EMBROIDERED SKIRT

... this impertinent garment.

No one took any notice of him. They were all too busy making money and having fun.

BEFORE THE PLAY

It was an exciting time. A new king was on the throne and change was in the air.

HAH HAH!
OO-SIR HENRY!
TINKLE TINKLE!

GRUMBLE... MUTTER... MUTTER...

An exciting time - provided you were part of it. Catholics felt totally left out.

This was the period when William Shakespeare wrote some of his greatest plays, put on in the new Globe theatre, south of the Thames. Theatres were typical of the time - exciting, but a little dangerous, the haunts of strutting young men with swords at their sides. It was said to be unwise to take your wife or sweetheart. A young thug might deliberately insult her, so that you would have to challenge him to a fight. Being an expert swordsman, he could then kill you and add another notch to his sword hilt. Swords were important. A sword was the sign of a gentleman, as was being good with it.

Catholics felt left out, but there must still have been quite a few Catholic swordsmen among the audiences which watched Shakespeare's plays - although any Catholics would have had to keep very quiet about their religion. The five youngish men who started the Gunpowder Plot were just the sort to go to the theatre:

Robert Catesby, Tom Wintour, Jack Wright, Thomas Percy and Guy Fawkes were all expert swordsmen and it's quite likely that they all drank in the same pubs and inns as Shakespeare and his friends.

THE PLAY BEGINS

The Plot began on Sunday 20 May 1604, when a very special meeting took place in a private room in the Duck and Drake tavern in the Strand area of London. Robert Catesby had called the meeting to discuss a plan which he'd recently dreamed up. If his plan succeeded, it would right the wrongs of Catholics at a stroke - if it failed, well ...

Catesby invited Wintour, Wright, Percy and Guy Fawkes to his meeting because each of them had the the right courage and skills for the job. Mostly they were big, fit men - fighters. And all of them were dedicated Catholics.

The plan was absolutely ruthless: to blow up the House of Lords at the opening of the next session of Parliament, when Lords, members of the House of Commons, the King and his young son would all be present. If little Prince Charles didn't go to Parliament with his father and elder brother, he would be grabbed and dealt with separately. Meanwhile there would be a Catholic uprising and Princess Elizabeth, James's daughter, would be kidnapped and made into a puppet queen. More than three hundred people would die in the explosion, including friends and relations of those present at the meeting in the Duck and Drake. The opening of Parliament was scheduled for 7 February 1605, less than a year away.

Catesby had already approached his friends one by one. When first told of the plan, several of them had been doubtful. As well as the risk to themselves, if it failed things would get far worse for Catholics than at present. Catesby had reassured them:

... the nature of the disease required so sharp a remedy.

Catesby was a very persuasive talker. He convinced them all. In the Duck and Drake, the five swore on a prayer book that they would keep the plot a secret. Then, after they'd finished their meeting, they went through to the next-door room and heard mass from a Catholic priest, Father Gerard, who was a friend of Catesby's. Gerard probably knew nothing of what they were plotting.

BEATUS VIR QUI TIMET DOMINUM, IN MANDATIS EJUS VOLET NIMIS!

AMEN!

PUBLIC ENEMY NO.1

ROBERT CATESBY (1573-1605).
'Robin' Catesby was six foot tall, well built and handsome. His father was Sir William Catesby of Warwickshire, a recusant. As we've seen, Robin had charm by the bucketful. As his relative Lord Monteagle put it:

... the only sun that must ripen our harvest.

A deadly charm as it turned out, since it was this charm more than anything else which persuaded most other members of the Gunpowder Plot to join him - and brought about their destruction.

..CALL ME ROBIN!

OK, OK!

THANK YOU, JOHN!

49

PUBLIC ENEMY NO.2

JACK WRIGHT (1568-1605) Jack Wright was one of Catesby's closest friends. He was tall and heavily built and was thought to be the best swordsman in England. His family were Catholic and he went to the same school in York as Guy Fawkes, who was two years younger.

PUBLIC ENEMY NO.3

TOM WINTOUR (1571-1606) Tom Wintour was short, stocky, clever - and fit. One of his uncles had been a Catholic priest who was hung, drawn and quartered back in 1586. Tom had fought in the English army against Spain in the Netherlands, he also fought in France and perhaps against the Turks. He could speak Spanish and French. When young he wasn't very religious, but that changed as he grew older.

See page 107.

PUBLIC ENEMY NO.4

THOMAS PERCY (1560-1605)

Thomas Percy was older than the others, and looked older still because his hair went white early in life. He was very tall, clever and built like a bull. In his youth he:

... relied much on his sword and his personal courage.

A bit of a wild man in fact. He was also a difficult character, a 'subtle, flattering, dangerous knave' as someone said. He was a distant relative of Henry Percy, the Catholic Earl of Northumberland.

SO — WHAT WERE YOU SAYING ABOUT ME BEING TOO OLD TO FIGHT?... SPEAK UP — I'VE LEFT MY EAR TRUMPET AT HOME!

NNG!

AND PUBLIC ENEMY NO.5 - THE GUY (OR GUIDO) ON YOUR BONFIRE

GUY FAWKES (1570-1606)

Guy Fawkes had thick brown hair and a stylish brown beard. He was tall and strong and a handy man with a sword. He converted to Catholicism when young, and around 1590, he joined the Spanish army in the Netherlands, fighting Protestants. He had nearly fifteen years experience of soldiering behind him when Catesby contacted him. Catesby asked Guy to join the Plot as explosives expert. An additional attraction was that Guy had been out of the country for so long that his face was unknown to the English authorities.

Guy had never believed that James would be kind to Catholics. In July 1603, soon after James took up his crown, Guy had visited Spain to try to persuade the Spanish authorities to back an invasion of England. Unfortunately, the Spanish had already been lulled by James's soft words. They were hoping for a peace treaty, not a war. The only thing Guy took back from his visit was a new name - from now on he chose to be known as 'Guido'.

WHAT A LOT OF PLOTTERS

It's all very well blowing things up. Even nowadays, if five terrorists blew up every building in Britain, they still wouldn't be able to form a government. All they would create would be a lot of rubble. Governments need *large numbers of people* to back them otherwise they don't stand a chance. Five plotters weren't enough to start a general Catholic uprising.

PUBLIC ENEMY No.6

ROBERT KEYES (1565-1606)

Robert Keyes was invited to join the plot in October 1604. Keyes was tall with a red beard and a good man with a sword. His father was a Protestant but his mother was a Catholic. He followed his mother's religion.

WE NEED MORE GOOD MEN - MEN DEDICATED TO THE FAITH - LIKE YOU! JOIN OUR NOBLE BAND, ROBERT!

'OD'S WOUNDS, I'M YOUR MAN, ROBIN - I'LL DO IT!

...THERE IS A DRESS CODE THOUGH!.. ER, YOUR HAT?...

PUBLIC ENEMY No.7

THOMAS BATES (?-1606)

Thomas Bates joined the Plot on 4 December 1604. Bates was a gentleman servant of Catesby. As such he had his own armour and an under servant of his own. Being part of the Catesby family as it were, he was bound to see what the plotters were up to so it was best to include him.

TOO TIGHT, DOBBS!

SORRY, SIR!

IS HE SOUND? CAN WE TRUST HIM? AND WHAT ABOUT HIS SERVANT?

WE HAVE NO CHOICE, ROBERT! BY THE WAY - LOVE THE HAT!

Public enemy No.8

ROBERT WINTOUR
(1568-1606)
Robert Wintour,
elder brother of Tom, joined the
Plot on 25 March 1605. He
was fit, a reliable friend and a
devout Catholic.

Public enemy No.9

KIT WRIGHT (1570-1605)
Kit (Christopher) Wright,
younger brother of
Jack, also joined the Plot on
25 March 1605. Like Jack,
Kit was tall and strong, a good
fighter and a devout Catholic.

Public enemy No.10

JOHN GRANT (C.1570-1606)
John Grant was a
brother-in-law of the
Wintours, a scholarly man, but
tough beneath the surface. He
too joined the Plot on
25 March 1605. Grant was to
be in charge of the capture of
large war horses from the
stable of Warwick Castle near
his own house. War horses
would be needed for the
general uprising.

ye PLOT PUZZLE...

CHECK OUT WHAT YOU KNOW ABOUT THE
GUNPOWDER PLOTTERS AND THEIR TIMES...

1. WHAT WAS A
   FARTHINGALE?

   A. A PADDED BOLSTER

   B. SMALL BEER

   C. A COAT OF ARMS

2. IN WHICH PUB
   DID THE PLOTTERS
   FIRST MEET?

   A. PIG AND WHISTLE

   B. DUCK AND DRAKE

   C. RAT AND TORTOISE

3. WHAT WOULD YOU
   DEFEND YOURSELF WITH
   DURING A DUEL?

   A. AN ONLOOKER

   B. A PET HAMSTER

   C. CLOAK AND DAGGER

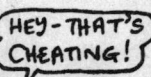

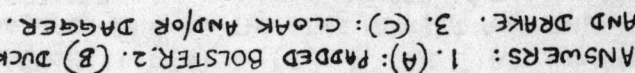

ANSWERS: 1. (A): PADDED BOLSTER. 2. (B) DUCK
AND DRAKE. 3. (C): CLOAK AND/OR DAGGER.

55

SALISBURY'S SPY SECRETS

The KING'S RIGHT-HAND MAN, LORD SALISBURY, PROBABLY KNEW THAT SOME SORT OF PLOT WAS AFOOT - THERE USUALLY WAS! SO HE USED A NETWORK OF SPIES TO HELP HIM KEEP TABS ON TROUBLE MAKERS. WOULD YOU HAVE BEEN A GOOD SPY?...

1. WOULD YOU RECOGNISE A 'MASS KIT'? IT'S A...
   A. SORT OF SHOTGUN
   B. PRIEST'S HOLY EQUIPMENT
   C. JESUIT'S FOOTBALL STRIP

ON ME HEAD!

EEK! SWISH! SWISH! SNICK! SWISH! SNICK! SNICK! SNICK! SNICK! SWISH!

HAH! SO MUCH FOR ARROWS! NOW FOR SWORDS!

2. WHO IS THE BEST SWORDSMAN IN ENGLAND?
   A. ROBIN HOOD
   B. MACK THE KNIFE
   C. JACK WRIGHT

3. USE THE WORDS ON PAGE 48 TO DECODE THIS SECRET MESSAGE:

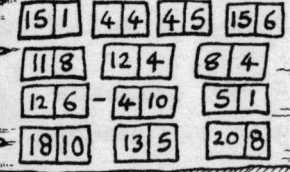

15 1	4 4	4 5	15 6
11 8	12 4	8 4	
12 6	- 4 10	5 1	
18 10	13 5	20 8	

SECURITY MATTERS

Nowadays it would be impossible for someone to lease a room near to a building as important to the government as the House of Lords, let alone directly beneath it. Secret service agents would pounce almost as soon as you made your first enquiry. But in the rabbit warren of the old palace of Westminster in 1605 there were no such problems. The seventeenth century wasn't very security conscious.

In June 1604, while Catesby was busy recruiting new plotters, Thomas Percy rented a 'house' in the Palace of Westminster, and Guido Fawkes began to live there, disguised as Percy's servant and under the false name of John Johnson.

The 'house' which the plotters rented was little more than a room, but it was right next door to the chamber of the House of Lords. In fact there was an unused door into the chamber. The 'house' was so small that there was no room for anyone else to sleep there apart from 'John Johnson'.

Then on 23 December 1604, the government announced that the opening of the new parliament would be delayed until October 1605. This gave the plotters time to lease a 'cellar' directly beneath the House of Lords, which they did on 25 March 1605. (They gave up on plans to tunnel underneath.)

The 'cellar' which the plotters leased ran beneath the House of Lords and their own little 'house', both of which were really on the first floor. It had once been the old medieval kitchen of the Palace of Westminster and had been used for storing coal by its previous tenant. It was so unused and ramshackle-looking that people hardly noticed that it was there.

POWDER!

Once the cellar had been rented, it was time for 'John Johnson' to bring in the gunpowder. Most of it was sneaked inside in small barrels, called firkins. The Palace of Westminster is right by the River Thames, so it wasn't too difficult to carry the powder from boats moored at the bottom of Parliament Stairs about forty yards away. Since there were several pubs in the area, and amid the general bustle, a man carrying a barrel was nothing unusual. Between 25 March and 20 July, thirty-six barrels of gunpowder were packed into the cellar and hidden beneath a pile of firewood.

Enough to blow the House of Lords to kingdom come.

GUNPO-

MORE THAN YOU NEED TO KNOW

AN EXPLOSIVE SUBJECT

Nowadays, explosives experts say that gunpowder isn't an explosive at all really: it's just a substance that burns very rapidly, 'deflagrates' to use the specialist word. At best, it's officially described as a 'low explosive'.

Well, gunpowder may be non-explosive or low-explosive by comparison with modern high explosives, but by the standards of the seventeenth century it was quite explosive enough. At the height of a gunpowder 'explosion' temperatures reach 2,100-2,700° C. Thirty-six barrels would have made a very powerful bomb.

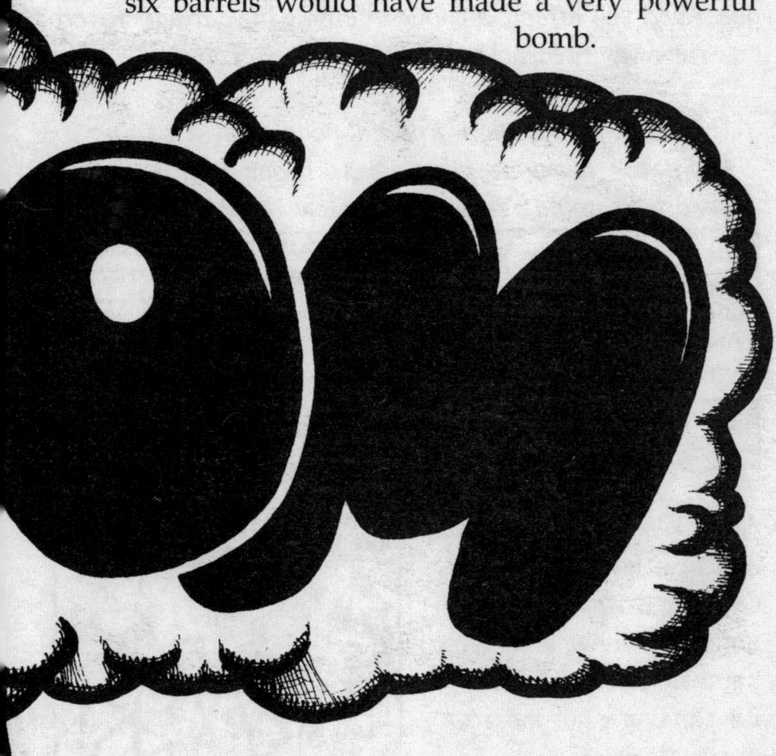

THE TALE OF GUNPOWDER

AD 500s: Firecrackers were first used in China to scare off devils. The firecrackers were simply green bamboo canes. When thrown on a fire, the air inside the sections would expand and explode outwards in a series of loud bangs.

The famous thirteenth-century traveller Marco Polo described the effect, although he may have exaggerated how far away firecrackers could be heard from:

> They burn with such a dreadful noise that it can be heard ten miles at night, and anyone who is not used to it could easily go into a swoon or even die.

AD 800s: When gunpowder was first invented by the Chinese, it was probably used as a replacement for bamboo firecrackers and for the same purpose: to scare off devils.

AD 1044: The earliest recipe for gunpowder yet to be discovered was written during the Sung dynasty. The recipe includes saltpetre, charcoal and sulphur, the basic ingredients of gunpowder from that day to this, as well as other more exotic ingredients.

GOOD — GOOD! SO... A TENTH PART OF THE YELLOW POWDER, A SIXTH OF THE BLACK — THE REST IS THE WHITE CRYSTALS!..

HAH! GOTCHA!

ARGH! FIRE-LANCES! RUN!

C.AD 1133: Twenty 'fire lances' were used in the defence of the city of Te-an, near Hankow. The firelances were probably bamboo canes, perhaps filled with a mixture of gunpowder and other dangerous substances. They produced a jet of searing flame.

C.1130s: A Chinese writer of the same period, Wei Hsing, described the launching of 'firestones' containing a 'fire drug'. There is no evidence that the 'firestones' were launched with the aid of gunpowder, instead they could have been thrown by a catapult or some other device. The firestones may have been 'Greek fire', a substance which sends out large flames, or they may have contained gunpowder, or both.

HAH! GOTCHA AGAIN!

ARGH! RUN! FIRESTONES!

EEK!

'C.' stands for *circa*, Latin for 'around'. 'C.' before a date means it's only approximate.

1245: Giovanni del Carpine, the first European to visit the Mongol Empire, described how the Mongols used a type of 'Greek fire' containing human fat. It could only, he said, be put out with wine or beer. By this date the Chinese were definitely using both gunpowder and Greek fire in warfare.

1267: The first named European known to learn of gunpowder was the English monk and scientist, Roger Bacon, who wrote a description of it in 1267. Knowledge of this new substance would have been brought to Europe from China by travellers such as Marco Polo, or perhaps his uncles. Marco Polo himself visited China slightly later.

1280: A recipe for gunpowder was written by the Arab scientist Hasan Al'Rammah. The Arabs learned of gunpowder at the same time as the Europeans or slightly before. It may have been Arabs who first developed a quick-burning type of gunpowder which could shoot 'bullets'.

SALTPETRE

Gunpowder is a mixture of three ingredients: ground up charcoal, saltpetre and sulphur, as the Chinese discovered. Early Chinese recipes used quite small quantities of saltpetre, which meant that their gunpowder didn't explode, or burn, quickly enough to shoot bullets. To do that, and to make the sort of gunpowder used in the Gunpowder Plot, as much as 60% of the gunpowder mixture should be saltpetre.

The word 'saltpetre' comes from the Latin *sal petrae*, meaning 'salt of rock'. If you have an old brick

basement or cellar it's quite likely you will find saltpetre in white crystals growing from the walls - but only in small quantities. Saltpetre has always been the hardest ingredient of gunpowder to manufacture.

Saltpetre is a *nitrate*, a salt of *nitric acid*, as is fertiliser (which is why terrorists often use fertiliser to make their bombs), and the most useful form of saltpetre for making gunpowder is *potassium nitrate*. Nitrates are produced as a product of the rotting process of animal and vegetable waste. When gardeners rot old vegetables on their compost heaps, they're not just being mucky; the end result, compost, is rich in nitrates.

Saltpetre occurs naturally in the soil since it's produced from rotting vegetable and animal matter. But only in some parts of the world does it occur in collectible quantities - and not in Europe.

For years saltpetre was imported from the Ganges valley in India, where vast amounts of human and animal manure rotted in just the right kind of soil to be easily collected and processed.

Despite the trade in Indian saltpetre, enough of it was never imported to meet the demands of warlike European states. The answer was to produce saltpetre locally. All over Europe, rulers tried to encourage manufacture of the stuff. 'Petering' grew into a major industry and 'saltpetre men' were always looking for new sources. English saltpetre men asked permission to scrape the floors of churches because:

Women pisse in their seats which causes excellent salt petre.

Salt, Peter?

It was in 1561 that a German called Gerard Honricke decided to start a saltpetre 'farm' in England. His recipe survives. It involved mixing human and animal manure, quicklime (as in plaster of Paris) and lime from oyster shells, with urine:

... from persons whiche drink either wyne or strong beers.

A drinker's urine contains more potassium than sodium, compared to his more sober friends, and it's *potassium nitrate* which is needed for gunpowder, not *sodium nitrate*. The mixture was to be left in a heap and turned once a fortnight for at least a year while it rotted. At each turning, the brick floor and walls would be swept clean of the saltpetre which:

... will hang like snow upon them.

The next job was to remove unwanted salts. This was done by dissolving the saltpetre in water, boiling off a lot of the water and then cooling the remainder. After the boiling was over, the nitrates would collect in the bottom of the vessel as it cooled, leaving other, undesirable salts, such as sodium chloride (common table salt), in the water. Table salt ruined gunpowder, to such an extent that experienced gunners used to

taste their powder to make sure it wasn't 'salty'. Another German, Lazarus Erker, even recommended collecting the table salt from the saltpetre water and selling it.

Other stages in the process allowed the manufacturer to remove unwanted nitrates, finally leaving potassium nitrate, the one which was needed. The other nitrates absorbed water too easily and would stop the gunpowder from catching light and exploding.

Got any corns?

Gunpowder was useful not just because it exploded, but because it didn't explode when you didn't want it to, quite important when you come to think about it. You can shake gunpowder around, in fact give it quite a hammering, and it won't go off. It's ideal for carting about with armies, or in your gunpowder pouch if you're out shooting.

Without fire to make it go off, it's almost harmless. But of course - it won't catch light if it's damp. Gunpowder which is left alone too long in a damp place, such as a cellar beneath the House of Lords, will tend to become useless.

Early gunpowder manufacturers managed to limit the problem of dampness by mixing charcoal, saltpetre and sulphur to make gunpowder, then kneading the gunpowder into a paste with water. The paste was squidged into large lumps, called *knollen*, which were then left to dry. The outside of the *knollen* absorbed moisture but the inside would tend to remain dry. When the time came to use the *knollen* they were broken down into smaller lumps or grains with a pestle and mortar.

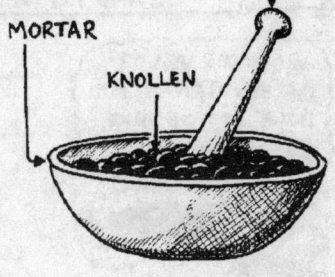

Knollen led to another discovery: the smaller the grains, the bigger the explosion. This was due to the fact that a gunpowder explosion is really a very quick fire. It burns first on the surface of each grain after which the fire spreads to the centre. The smaller the grains, the more total surface area to start with and the quicker the fire. Manufacturers began to squeeze gunpowder paste through sieves to produce different sizes of grains, a process called 'corning'. The smallest grains were for muskets and pistols and the largest were for long barrelled cannon. Long cannon were likely to burst if the explosion in the barrel was too fierce and quick.

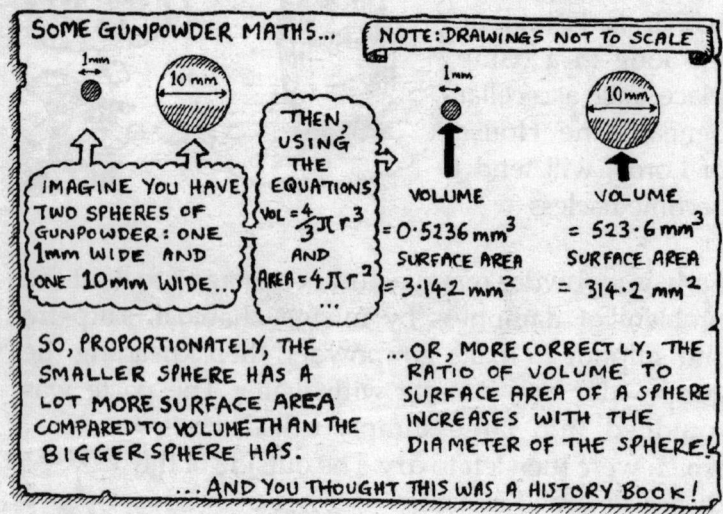

Guy Fawkes probably chose the large-grained variety. It would have been less easily affected by damp - and he collected enough of it to make sure of a very large bang anyway.

PLOT CROSS FUN

READ THE SECRET MESSAGE, THEN SOLVE THE PUZZLE

The crossword grid spells out:
THE PEN
TY FOR WRI
TING
THIS BO
EHUNG
DRAWN AND
ARTER
D!

Down letters: INTY, KNOB, PAL, LINOTNOT G, QUE, etc.

NOW IMAGINE THE CROSSWORD ABOVE IS BLANK...

CLUES ACROSS

1: JOHN ____ WAS A PLOTTER (5)

4: A MONTH TO REMEMBER (8)

7: A MORE POWERFUL TYPE OF BOMB (4)

8: [SEE 3 DOWN]

11: THE 'BYE' AND 'RIDOLFI' WERE EXAMPLES OF THESE (5)

12: WHAT GUNPOWDER DOES (8)

13: SHE CASTS SPELLS (5)

CLUES DOWN

1: HAND WEAPON (3)

2: ____ WINTOUR (3)

3 & 8 ACROSS: GUY FAWKES WORRIED ABOUT THIS (3, 6)

5: GUNPOWDER WAS PACKED IN THESE (7)

6: ____ CECIL (6)

9: CRIMINALS AT LARGE (7)

10: TINDER ____ (3)

11: THE WHITE-HAIRED PLOTTER (5)

PUZZLE: THE HATCHED ▨ LETTERS SPELL OUT ONE OF THE CHARACTERS IN THIS BOOK! [ANSWERS ON PAGE 122]

CONFESSION SESSIONS

GIVING THE GAME AWAY

THE SEAL OF THE CONFESSIONAL

In late July 1605, having stashed the gunpowder, Guy Fawkes returned to Flanders (part of what is now Belgium) to lie low for a while and to search out supporters among fellow Catholic exiles.

Then something bad happened: a few days after Guy Fawkes left the country, Robert Catesby 'confessed' about the entire plot to a Catholic priest he knew, called Father Tesimond!

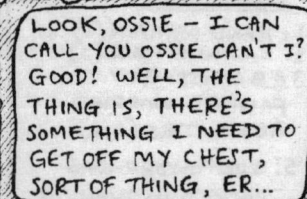

Confession is a Catholic thing. Catholics are meant to 'confess' all their sins to a Catholic priest regularly and to ask God for forgiveness, so Catesby was only doing what Catholics are meant to do.

Confession is always completely secret: by the rules of the 'seal of the confessional' the priest must never tell anyone else. So there was no danger to the plotters – but, as it turned out, there was danger for the priests.

Father Tesimond was horrified by what Catesby had confessed to him. He saw immediately that Catesby's plan was sheer madness. Catesby and his band of Catholic hotheads were about to kill a lot of innocent people and all the Catholics in England would suffer for their crime. Worst of all, poor Father Tesimond couldn't tell anyone because of the 'seal of the confessional'!

On the other hand, could Father Tesimond really keep the horrifying news to himself? Surely, if he didn't tell anyone, then he too would be guilty of the deaths of innocent people?

Actually there was a way round the problem. Father Tesimond visited another Catholic priest, Father Garnet - and 'confessed' the whole thing to him, which was allowed. Now they both knew about it.

The only trouble was: Father Garnet was also bound by the seal of the confessional. Neither priest could warn anyone else, not directly anyway. Perhaps theoretically, all the Catholic priests in the country could have ended up confessing about the plot to each other, but even that wouldn't have solved the problem: they still couldn't act in a way which would break the seal of the confessional.

THE REAL PUBLIC ENEMY

Father Garnet was no ordinary priest. He was leader of the English *Jesuits* and therefore Father Tesimond's superior. Jesuits were an organisation of Catholic priests, run on semi-military lines. They were dedicated to spreading Catholicism and they were very good at it. When becoming Jesuits, they all swore to 'go wherever the Pope chose to send them', an oath which lay at the heart of their problems in England. When captured, English Catholic priests were usually asked the 'bloody question':

> *Whose side would you take if the Bishop of Rome (the Pope) or other prince by his authority should invade the realm ...*

In other words: which side are you on? Take your choice - Pope or country. As far as Protestants were concerned it was *obvious* which side the Jesuits were on. To Protestants, English Jesuits, and their leader in particular, were the *real* public enemy No.1.

The Jesuits weren't helped by some of their fellow priests, who deliberately gave them a bad name. From the 1590s, English Catholics had been split down the middle: Jesuits on one side and their opponents, the 'Appellants', on the other. Appellants wanted to come to terms with the government and they believed that the Jesuits were a dangerous nuisance. The government itself recognised the difference between the two sides. In 1602, a royal proclamation called the Jesuits 'traitorous', but gave the Appellants a chance to negotiate.

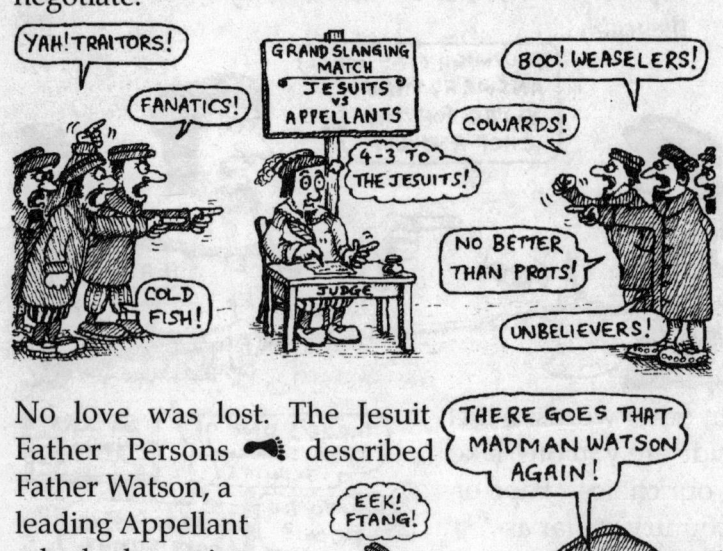

No love was lost. The Jesuit Father Persons 🐾 described Father Watson, a leading Appellant who had a squint, as:

... so wrong shapen and of so bad and blinking aspect that he looketh nine ways at once.

In 1595, Father Persons had published the *Book of Succession*, 'proving' among other things that James should not become King of England. This didn't help either.

To be fair, Father Persons was one of the most extreme Jesuits. When an old man in Rome, he relished talking about the sufferings of Appellants who had been caught and executed. Father Garnet would never have done that - although he never got the chance.

STOP THE PLOT - OR NOT!

On 28 July, the opening of Parliament was put off yet again, this time to 5 November. That gave Father Garnet an extra month in which to stop the plot, ten weeks in all. He sent messages to Rome, hinting that something violent was being planned, but not saying what it was since that would break the seal of the confessional, his information coming as it did from Catesby's confession to Father Tesimond. Garnet asked that the Pope make a special declaration against the use of violence by English Catholics. If the Pope spoke, the Plotters should listen.

Once his messages were on their way to Rome, Father Garnet went back to life as normal, and towards the end of August he went off on a pilgrimage to Wales. It's difficult not to think that he could have done more:

Yes, impious Garnet for the traitors prayed
Pricked and pushed forward those he might have stayed
Being accessory to this damned intent
Which with one word this Jesuit might prevent.

That was a Protestant poem, written after the plot was uncovered. Meanwhile the plot gathered steam. At a secret meeting in Bath sometime in August, the conspirators decided that they needed to recruit yet more members. They gave Catesby a free hand to 'call in whom he thought best'.

PUBLIC ENEMY No.11

AMBROSE ROOKWOOD (1578?-1606)

Ambrose Rookwood was short but brave. He was also rich and he loved riding. Catesby recruited Rookwood (29 September) because he kept a stable full of horses at his great house at Coldham in the east of England. On Catesby's advice, Rookwood plus horses moved to a large house near Stratford, where he would be near his fellow plotters. They would need the horses when the time came to seize Princess Elizabeth, James's daughter and their future puppet queen, and to start the uprising.

SO - YOU'RE WITH US THEN, AMBROSE?

I'M YOUR MAN, ROBIN!

SPOTON! AND YOU'LL HAVE TO MEET OUR FRIEND JOHN - HE'S A HORSE-CHAPPY TOO!

ER... 'HORSE-CHAPPY'??

PUBLIC ENEMY No.12

FRANCIS TRESHAM (1568-1605)

Francis Tresham was a useless choice for a plotter. About the only thing in his favour was that he was Catesby's cousin and he was a Catholic. He had a reputation for being untrustworthy, and, when young, he'd been sent to prison for a violent attack on a man and his pregnant daughter who owed money to the Tresham family. Tresham later claimed that he disagreed with the whole idea of the plot when Catesby tried to recruit him on 14 October 1605 - but then he would say that, wouldn't he? In any event, he did nothing to warn the authorities of what was afoot.

IT WASN'T MY IDEA - OH, NO! I DIDN'T AGREE WITH ANY OF IT! HONEST!

RUBBISH, TRESHAM! YOU'RE A PLOTTER! YOU'VE EVEN GOT A PLOTTER'S HAT!

PLOTTER NO.13 - THE LAST.

SIR EVERARD DIGBY (1578-1606)

Digby was tall, handsome and generous. He had riches, a lovely wife and he was well-known at court: in fact, he had everything to live for. Unfortunately, although brought up as Protestants, both he and his young wife had been converted to Catholicism by Father Gerard. It's possible that Catesby didn't tell Digby the full extent of the horror which had been planned for Parliament when he recruited him on 21 October. Digby provided money, arms and horses for the planned uprising and arranged for a 'meeting' of armed Catholic gentlemen for 5 November. This 'meeting' was planned to be the start of the general uprising. Also, Digby knew how to behave towards royalty. It would be his job to look after Princess Elizabeth after her capture.

... SO - WITH GOD'S GOOD GRACE - AND YOUR HELP, SIR EVERARD - OUR PLAN WILL SUCCEED!

YOU'VE CONVINCED ME, ROBIN! WITH YOUR EYE FOR DETAIL, SURELY NOTHING COULD GO WRONG!

JESUIT JOBSEARCH

HOW GOOD A SECRET CATHOLIC PRIEST WOULD YOU BE? NOTE THE DESCRIPTIONS THAT FIT YOU BEST ON THIS JOB APPLICATION FORM, THEN CHECK HOW YOU DID ON PAGE 123 !...

1. HEIGHT

A. TALL

B. MEDIUM

C. SHORT

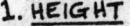

2. CONVERSATION

A. QUIET

B. ABLE TO KEEP A SECRET

C. LOUD-MOUTHED

3. INTELLIGENCE

A. VERY CLEVER

B. AVERAGE

C. STUPID

4. COURAGE

A. VERY BRAVE

B. COULD COPE PERHAPS

C. WIMPISH

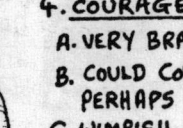

5. APPEARANCE

A. VERY FASHIONABLE

B. SMARTLY DRESSED

C. SCRUFFY

6. LANGUAGES

A. GOOD

B. OK

C. POOR

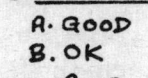

81

SUPPER TIME

Guy Fawkes returned to London in late August. He visited the cellar beneath the House of Lords with Tom

Wintour. While he'd been away, the gunpowder had got damp, 'dank' as Wintour described it. The two men brought fresh gunpowder and fresh firewood as a screen to place on top of it.

Summer faded into autumn. The plotters held excited meetings, often over supper, in the Midlands and in various London taverns, including the Mitre in Bread Street and the Irish Boy in the Strand.

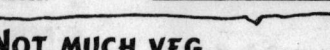

NOT MUCH VEG

The diet of a gentleman at that time consisted mainly of meat. Being large, fit men, the plotters no doubt ate a lot of it during their suppers. A typical meal would have included beef or mutton and often cheese, with bread and beer. No one ever drank water with their food. Fridays were different: it was compulsory to serve fish rather than meat on Fridays, a regulation brought in by Elizabeth I to help the fishing industry.

Taverns were very public places where cutthroats mingled with sword-dangling dandies who wore puffed out pantaloons and bowed elaborately to each other. It's amazing that the plotters kept their secret at all.

In fact, Jacobean London was still Tudor London in most respects. The plotters were part of that world of dandies and swordsmen. For instance, Shakespeare's friend the poet and playwright Ben Jonson was at their supper at the Irish Boy - and Jonson had swung swords with the best of them. He'd fought in Flanders and had once killed a man in a duel. Jonson later claimed not to have overheard anything suspicious.

London was dangerous at night. There was no public street lighting. Street lights were provided by private citizens outside their own houses. At night the streets were the haunt of robber bands and no citizen ventured out without a sword and a lantern. At midnight the watchmen called:

Twelve o'clock, look to your locks,
Your fire and your light,
And so good night.

Not that the plotters had much to fear. Robbers would have looked for easier prey than a group of large, determined men, among them the best swordsman in England. The plotters had had special swords made for themselves, of Spanish steel, their blades engraved with the motto:

The Passion of Christ

CLASH!!

DEATH TO THE PROTESTANTS!

FINAL PLANS

5 November was coming up fast. All the plotters must have known in their hearts that rich, powerful, Protestant London wasn't going to cave in as a result of a single bomb planted by just thirteen men, however large and however important the target. After all, London was the largest city in Europe and to the vast majority of its huge population even the word 'Catholic' was a term of abuse. And if London stood firm against the plotters, what hope that the rest of the country would rise up in rebellion?

WHAT IF SOMETHING GOES WRONG?...

...PLOT... PLOT... ...PLOT... PLOT...

ARE WE HEROES — OR VILLAINS?...

DO SO MANY REALLY HAVE TO DIE?...

But the plotters lived in a world where bravery and honour mattered more than life or even victory. Brave men and soldiers don't admit the possibility of defeat immediately before a battle. The plotters closed their eyes to the hopelessness of what they were doing. They went ahead and planned the final details.

Guy Fawkes would light the fuse then leave the cellar quickly. If all went according to plan, he would be half way across the River Thames in a boat by the time the bomb went off. Once on the other side he would make his way to the coast and cross the Channel to Flanders. Meanwhile the uprising would have started in the Midlands and Princess Elizabeth would have been kidnapped and declared Queen. And while the uprising was, hopefully, sweeping the country, Guy would be in Flanders, where he would try to persuade its Spanish rulers to back the English Catholics in their hour of need.

AND FINAL DOUBTS

There was no hesitation and there were no doubts - not on the surface at any rate. But underneath, the plotters must have worried that what they were about to do was what it really was: cold-blooded murder. What seems to have particularly worried Catesby was the number of Catholic lords and members of the House of Commons who would die in the explosion. On 15 October he met Catholic Viscount Montague who had once employed Guy Fawkes to wait at his table  and was a leader of the Catholic community. Catesby tried to hint to Montague that it would be best not go to the opening of Parliament in November, but all he could safely say without giving the game away was:

I think your Lordship takes no pleasure to be there.

Montague agreed that he didn't take pleasure to be there - but he didn't take the hint either.

Then, on Saturday 26 October, just nine days away from Big Bang, someone's doubts finally got the better of them - or so it seems. That night a badly-written letter was slipped into the hand of Thomas Ward, one of the servants of Lord Monteagle, outside Lord Monteagle's London house, while Monteagle was

To wait at the table of a nobleman was an honourable thing to do and not work for a common servant. Kings were waited on by noblemen.

inside having supper with some friends. Monteagle was a Catholic who had recently converted to Protestantism. He was related to Catesby, to the Wright brothers and to Francis Tresham. That, presumably, was why he was contacted. This dramatic letter is now kept in the Public Records Office, in London. It blew the whole plot wide open:

> *My Lord, out of the love I bear to some of your friends, I have a care of your preservation. Therefore I would advise you, as you tender your life, to devise some excuse to shift of your attendance at this Parliament ... For though there be no appearance of any stir, yet I say they shall receive a terrible blow this Parliament ...*

GOTCHA!

THE FOURTH OF NOVEMBER ...
I'VE GOT A LETTER FOR YOU

The letter of betrayal was red hot. If Monteagle didn't tell the authorities about it immediately, he would be suspected of being on the side of the plotters. Especially so since he'd only recently become a Protestant, in order to get on and make money at court. It would be easy enough for an enemy to accuse him of still being a 'church papist', a secret Catholic. Monteagle had to prove he wasn't - and fast. He hurried round to the home of Robert Cecil, James's chief minister, with the letter clasped in his hand.

COOL HAND CECIL

Robert Cecil, Lord Salisbury, 'my dearest and trusty 10' as James used to call him in their private code, was only just over 1.6 metres tall (5ft. 3in.) and was a hunchback. He made up for his weakness by being a brilliant and very cunning politician. He had been powerful for years. Before becoming James's chief minister, he'd been chief minister to Elizabeth I, and it was him who'd arranged for James to be her successor as ruler of England. After James, Cecil was the most powerful man in the country.

Cecil read the letter with interest. He'd been expecting something like this, because his spies had warned him that the Catholics were up to something, although they didn't know what. Cool as a cucumber, he decided to do nothing - for the time being. There were still ten days until the opening of Parliament. He would wait and watch for the plot to 'ripen' in the hope of finding out who was behind it.

James meanwhile was out hunting the deer of Essex. His pleasure was to career flat-out over the countryside after deer and other unfortunate creatures. In fact, he was a hunting fanatic and, although terrified of being murdered (with reason!), he was no coward. When he returned to London on Thursday 31 October, Cecil showed him the letter. James agreed that there should be no immediate search of the Houses of Parliament. The plot could 'ripen' further, and James would have to suffer increased fear of murder for a few days in order to find out who was behind it.

OH DEER!

Cruelty to animals was normal in Tudor and Jacobean England. Bear-baiting and cock-fighting were everyday activities. Most towns had a bull-baiting ring or 'bull ring' - it was thought that 'baiting' an animal, usually with dogs, before killing it, made the meat more tender 🐾. Monarchs and wealthy nobles kept 'deer parks' for hunting. When out hunting Elizabeth liked to seat herself comfortably and have the deer driven towards her so that she could shoot lots of them with a bow and arrow without getting up. James hunted on horseback so at least the deer had some chance of escaping!

THERE'S ONE!

AFTER IT!

TALLY-HO!

👣 This is actually the opposite of the case. Frightened animals give off the hormone adrenalin which makes meat less tender. Extreme fear at the moment of death can even lead to instant *rigor mortis* when the muscles seize up.

So now the authorities knew that there was a plot, but they didn't know who was doing the plotting. Meanwhile the plotters had a lucky break. Thomas Ward, Lord Monteagle's servant, the one who'd been passed the letter on Saturday 26 October, was the brother of plotter Kit Wright's wife! While Monteagle scuttled round to see Cecil, Ward sent a warning message to Catesby. He knew that Catesby and Kit Wright were close friends.

Having read Ward's note, Catesby and Tom Wintour accused Francis Tresham of writing the letter of betrayal, but Tresham convinced them that he was innocent. At this point Catesby, as leader of the Plot, should have called the whole thing off. Clearly someone had tried to betray them and might try again. But Catesby, being Catesby, kept on. He said that, since the letter didn't betray the plot in detail, it was no threat.

On 30 October, since no one told him not to, Guy Fawkes made a final inspection of the cellar. All was in order - or so it seemed.

Do you remember the 4th of November?

4 November 1605 was just another Monday. The citizens of London hauled themselves from their beds at the usual unearthly hour. Five o'clock was considered normal in those days. As usual, the apprentices were up before their masters to take down the shutters outside the shops, maids hurried to light fires in the bedrooms, schoolboys got ready for school and the ale houses opened their doors for business.

But beneath the surface, Monday 4 November was anything but normal. Thirteen desperate men were about to embark on a doomed adventure, and watching for them like a spider above its web was Robert Cecil, the hunchback Earl of Salisbury. One way or another, a lot of people were going to suffer.

Countdown to catastrophe

11.00am: Plotter Thomas Percy visits the house of his employer and distant relation, the Catholic Earl of Northumberland, just outside London, to check if there are any rumours about the plot. Everything seems to be peaceful.

5.00-6.00pm: Percy tells his fellow plotters Tom Wintour, Jack Wright and Robert Keyes that 'all is well', then he goes to his lodgings and gives orders for his horses to be made ready to leave very early the following morning.

Some time in the afternoon: Lord Suffolk, with Lord Monteagle and a few others, takes a casual look at the cellar beneath the House of the Lords. They notice a tall man standing in or near the cellar, and then leave, pretending not to have noticed anything suspicious.

10.00pm: Guy Fawkes visits Robert Keyes to collect a watch which Percy has left for him. He needs the watch to time the fuse for the bomb.

After 10.00pm: Robert Catesby sets out for the Midlands to take part in the uprising.

11.00pm: The last specially engraved sword of Spanish steel is delivered to one of the last men to join the Plot, Ambrose Rookwood.

93

THE MIDNIGHT HOUR

At around twelve midnight a second search party, headed by Sir Thomas Knevett, returned to the cellar below the House of Lords. This time, on James's orders, they searched it thoroughly.

This time they discovered thirty-six barrels of

gunpowder overlaid with iron bars to cause maximum destruction. Beside the barrels of gunpowder stood a tall man in a cloak and a dark hat with boots and spurs on as if ready for a journey. They arrested him. He gave his name as John Johnson, a servant of Thomas Percy. In his pocket they found his garters, a piece of touchwood and a tinder box ⬟ together with a watch.

Touchwood was very dry wood which would catch fire easily. Matches had not been invented. The *tinder box* would have contained flint and steel for striking a spark.

SCRAM!

While 'John Johnson' was tied up with his own garters and hauled off to a room in the Palace of Westminster for questioning, Westminster went into uproar. Servants ran hither and thither, senior politicians were roused from their beds for

the emergency. In no time the first arrest warrant was issued, for Thomas Percy whom the government already suspected and who was now known to be 'John Johnson's' master.

At about five in the morning of 5 November, realising from the hullabaloo that the game was up, Kit Wright raced round to warn Tom Wintour then on to Percy's lodgings, since Percy was most immediately in danger. Percy and Kit Wright then left town, their horses' hooves clattering through the dark and empty streets together. Percy called to a servant as he left:

I am undone.

Robert Keyes was next to leave. Dawn was just breaking over St. Paul's when he took to the road. That left Rookwood and Tom Wintour still in London. Rookwood had been asked to join the plot because he was such a good horseman. Now he proved the point.

He had already arranged for changes of horses to be ready for him along the way north so that he could join the uprising quickly once the bomb went off. He rode thirty miles in two hours to start with, overtaking Keyes at Highgate. In Bedfordshire he finally caught up with Thomas Bates and Jack Wright, and with Catesby, who had left at 10.00 pm the previous evening (see page 93).

Now, apart from poor Guy, only Tom Wintour was left in London. He wandered casually down to Westminster to see if things were really as bad as Kit Wright had told him, a pretty brave thing to do in the circumstances. Guards were stopping people in the road. Someone said:

There is a treason discovered in which the King and the Lords were to be blown up.

That convinced Wintour. He saddled his horse and left town for his brother's house at Huddington in Worcestershire.

TORTURE

OR - PULL THE OTHER ONE!

MAN OF IRON

Guy Fawkes was now on his own. Other men would have cracked under the pressure but not him. Smiling scornfully at his questioners, who included the King himself, Guy gave nothing away which would endanger his fellow plotters. He said his name was John Johnson and that was that. Far from showing regret, he defiantly told them that it was a shame that they had uncovered the plot:

> *The devil and not God was the discoverer.*

He also freely admitted that he had meant to murder the lot of them, and when James's Scottish cronies crowded into the room, he told them that he had intended:

To blow them all back into Scotland.

RACKED WITH GUILT

That evening Guy was taken to the Tower of London and probably locked in an underground cell next to the torture chamber. They searched him one last time (they can't have been very good at it) and this time they found a letter addressed to his real name, Guy Fawkes. His cover was blown.

James was a merciful ruler by the standards of his time, but his safety and the safety of the kingdom depended on finding out the names of Guy's fellow plotters. Seeing as how Guy hadn't yet given any useful information away, on 6 November James agreed to the use of torture:

> *The gentler tortures are to be used first unto him et sic per gradus ad ima tenditur (and so by degrees proceed to the worst) ...*

To the astonishment of his guards, Guy was so cool that he slept as if without any troubles, although he knew what was going to happen to him. Next morning, they probably started the torture session with manacles.

1. Clamp victim's wrists in iron gauntlets and tighten as required.

2. Remove wooden bench or stool and leave to dangle.

3. Leave dangling for several hours.

In Guy Fawkes's case it's likely that manacles, although horribly painful, weren't enough to make him talk. Sir Thomas Coke who was in charge of the torture probably put him to the rack.

The rack was horrific. Limbs were dislocated from their sockets, muscles and tendons torn and broken.

Thomas Norton, a previous torturer, once boasted that he stretched one victim:

... one good foot longer than God ever made him.

HAH HAH! YOU'LL BE NEEDING A LONG HOLIDAY NOW! IN THE HIGH SEASON! IN A STRETCHED LIMO MAYBE! OR A TUG-BOAT! HAH HAH!

Not even a man of iron, not even Guy, could stand up to the rack. At the end of 7 November, Guy began to talk. By the evening of Friday 8 November, he'd given away the names of his fellow plotters.

PAINFUL PLOT PUZZLE

FOLLOWING GUY FAWKES' CONFESSIONS, ROBERT CECIL HAS SENT HIS AGENTS A CODED LIST OF FIVE PLOTTERS. CAN YOU DECODE THEIR REAL NAMES?...

1. RACK WITH J.G!

2. AGUES IF KWOD!

COR!

3. BERTY BEATS!

4. TURN TIM-OOW!

5. CHOPS ARM, YET!

ye Powder Plotters

JUST MY LITTLE JOKE!

ANSWERS: 1. JACK WRIGHT. 2. GUIDO FAWKES. 3. ROBERT CATESBY. 4. TOM WINTOUR. 5. THOMAS PERCY.

GUNPOWDER BOOB

While Guy suffered alone, the rest of the plotters regrouped in the Midlands. On the evening of 5 November, Catesby, Tom Bates, the Wright brothers, Rookwood and Percy were joined by Robert Wintour and later by Sir Everard Digby, together with various other Catholic gentlemen collected along the way. There were now over fifty desperate Catholic horsemen loose in the Midlands.

They rode through the night, but losing men to left and right as the fainter-hearted left them. On the afternoon of 6 November, the remainder joined up with Tom Wintour at his brother's house at Huddington in Worcestershire. Next day at around three in the morning, they rode out into the rain.

There were now thirty-six of them - the same as the number of barrels of gunpowder which would have blown up the House of Lords if everything had worked out as it should have done.

They rode all the following day, and at night they took refuge at Holbeach, the Staffordshire house of one of the Catholics who had come to Digby's 'meeting'. By now the authorities were in hot pursuit with a force of two hundred armed men.

It was a wet, dreary, hopeless night, leaking like a rusty sieve. Digby went off to surrender to the authorities as did Robert Wintour, then Thomas Bates slipped away into the darkness. And worse was to follow. Having been on the run since early Tuesday morning, and it was now late on Wednesday night, Catesby and the others were utterly exhausted. Their gunpowder had got damp in the rain. In a confused, exhausted state of mind, they spread it in front of the fire to dry. A crazy thing to do. Predictably, a spark from the fire set the powder off.

Catesby and Rookwood were burned but not too badly, Henry Morgan who had joined them on Sunday was badly burned and John Grant was blinded. Now, apart from these four, only the Wright brothers, Thomas Percy and Tom Wintour were left. These eight were determined to fight to the bitter end. When Wintour asked the others what they meant to do, they answered:

We mean here to die.

The attack by the government forces started at eleven o'clock on the morning of Friday 8 November. Tom Wintour was shot first, in the arm.

Next, Jack Wright, and his brother Kit were both shot.

Then Ambrose Rookwood was wounded.

Catesby, Tom Wintour and Percy stood together at the door to the house. Catesby and Percy were both shot by the same musket ball.

Tom Wintour, Grant, Morgan and Rookwood were arrested. All of them were in a poor state due to gunpowder burns, gunshot wounds or both.

The Wright brothers and Percy died of their wounds soon after.

Catesby crawled inside to die. His body was found clutching a picture of the Virgin Mary .

Of the original plotters, only five now remained at large. Of them, Robert Keyes was soon caught, and Sir Everard Digby gave himself up on 10 November.

Thomas Bates was caught in Staffordshire.

Francis Tresham was arrested in London on the 12 November.

That left Robert Wintour and Stephen Littleton, a companion from the 'uprising'. They stayed free and on the run until the ninth of January, when they were betrayed by the cook at a house where they were hiding deep in rural Worcestershire .

 The Virgin Mary was the mother of Jesus and is a favourite subject of Catholic paintings.

Littleton, Henry Morgan and some others, who joined the uprising on 5 November, were later executed separately from the original plotters.

WHAT A TRIAL

On 27 January 1606, the trials of the remaining eight of the original plotters: Guy Fawkes, Robert and Thomas Wintour, Ambrose Rookwood, John Grant, Thomas Bates, Robert Keyes and Sir Everard Digby, were held in Westminster Hall, the great medieval hall which still stands beside the Houses of Parliament. (Francis Tresham had died in captivity.) They were made to stand on a platform where they could be seen by all, while James watched from a private room. Trials in the seventeenth century weren't trials as we understand the word today. Questioning to discover the truth took place beforehand and the 'trial' was simply a show trial, held to show that the accused were guilty.

| GUY FAWKES | ROBERT WINTOUR | TOM WINTOUR | AMBROSE ROOKWOOD | JOHN GRANT | THOMAS BATES | ROBERT KEYES | SIR EVERARD DIGBY |

Sir Everard Digby pleaded not guilty because this meant that he could make a speech. The other seven pleaded guilty. They all took tobacco throughout the trial - even though James had written a book denouncing it: *Counterblaste to Tobacco*.

106

A LONG SENTENCE

At the end of the day, as was predictable, all eight were pronounced guilty of high treason. The sentence of hanging drawing and quartering was described to them by Attorney-General, Sir Edward Coke:

1. Draw the prisoner backwards to execution at a horse's tail.

2. Hang him for a bit - but not too long.

3. Cut off his privy parts and burn them before his face.

4. Hack out the bowels and heart.

5. Chop off his head.

6. Publically expose parts of the body, to become 'prey to the fowls of the air'.

HANGING DRAWING AND QUARTERING

The executions took place over two days, on 30 and 31 January 1606.

Digby went first. He was only hanged for a short while so he was fully conscious when they cut him up. The executioner held his heart saying, as was customary: 'Here is the heart of a traitor', and Digby is said to have replied:

Thou liest.

Robert Wintour went quietly.

John Grant was blind from the explosion in Staffordshire. He had to be led to the scaffold.

Bates said he was sorry.

Tom Winter said he wasn't sorry. He was cut down quickly from the rope so he was still conscious when he was cut up.

Rookwood was allowed to hang until he was nearly dead.

Robert Keyes tried to jump off the scaffold and thus hang himself instantly. The rope broke. He was cut up while fully conscious.

Guy Fawkes himself was the last to die. He was very weak from the torture and his neck was broken by the hangman's rope - which was fortunate, given what he'd already endured.

109

GARNET GETS IT TOO

PRIEST IN A HOLE

NOSE VIPERS

Robert Cecil, James's chief minister, didn't particularly want to see Catholics 'die by the dozen' - unless they were guilty of treason. But Jesuits (see pages 74 and 75) got up his nose. Cecil thought that all Jesuits were:

... that generation of vipers.

From Cecil's point of view, because the Jesuit order of priests was dedicated to turning the world Catholic, it was a major threat to James's kingdom. The Gunpowder Plot gave him a chance to get rid of the Jesuits once and for all. He was determined that the plotters should give evidence against the Jesuits, whether the Jesuits were guilty or not. Under torture or the threat of torture, the plotters were asked again and again to say that Jesuits had been involved in the Plot from the beginning.

CONFESSION TIME (PART 2)

It's amazing what a bit of torture, or the threat of torture, will do. No Jesuits had been among the plotters and both Father Tesimond and Father Garnet had even tried to stop the Plot after they'd heard Catesby's confession (see page 72). No matter, before they were executed the plotters were 'persuaded' to admit that Jesuits had been involved all along.

9 November 1605: Guy Fawkes's third confession, after severe torture, named Father Gerard (see page 49) as having given the Holy Sacrament to the plotters after the oath of secrecy sworn in the Duck and Drake, back in May 1604.

23 November 1605: Tom Wintour's confession (which may have been forged) fingered Father Gerard and the little, lame maker of priest holes, Nicholas Owen (Little John), who was a Jesuit 'lay brother'.

 A *lay brother* is a monk who is not a priest.

29 November 1605: Francis Tresham's confession fingered Father Garnet for involvement in the start of a plot back in 1602. Tresham died of illness on 23 December. His head was chopped off his dead body.

GARNET'S THE ONE YOU WANT!

STOP SWEATING ON ME, TRESHAM!

HE WAS THE WEAKEST LINK!

GOOD-BYE!

WAS TESIMOND INVOLVED?

HE MIGHT HAVE BEEN...

LET ME USE THE HOT PINCERS, BOSS!

CLIP! CLIP!

4 December 1605: Thomas Bates's confession fingered Father Tesimond.

IF I SAY GERARD AND GARNET KNEW... WILL YOU LET ME OFF?..

WE MIGHT DO...

13 January 1606: another confession by Thomas Bates fingered Fathers Gerard and Garnet as well as Father Tesimond.

HOT PINCERS YET?

CLIP!

PRIESTS PICKED UP IN PRIESTHOLE POO DRAMA

After Thomas Bates's second confession, the government felt that it had enough evidence to 'prove' that Fathers Tesimond, Gerard and Garnet were guilty of treason. On 15 January 1606, a proclamation was issued calling for their capture. Of the three, Father Garnet, being leader of the English Jesuits, was by far the most important. He was described as:

... full faced, fat of body, of complexion fair, his forehead high on each side with a little hair thinning down ...

On the same day, Father Tesimond escaped to the continent by hiding in a cargo of dead pigs.

Two Jesuits, Fathers Strange and Singleton, had already been picked up on 7 November. They'd been on their way to warn Father Garnet that a plot had been uncovered. Priests all over the country went into deeper hiding. In December Father Garnet, with another priest Father Oldcorne and two lay brothers,

Little John and Ralph Ashley, moved to Hindlip Hall, in Worcestershire. Hindlip was riddled with priestholes and was one of the safest houses in the

country. Little John had built the priestholes, so he should know. It was safe, but far from comfortable: Garnet and Oldcorne's hole was so small that they couldn't stand up in it.

The authorities began their search of Hindlip Hall on 20 January 1606. The search went on for six days and it was very, very thorough. Walls were tapped, beds unmade, cupboards and chests searched, fires lit in fireplaces. Even so, no one was found. Not until, eventually, the four men were driven out of their hiding places by lack of food and by other discomforts.

Little John and Ashley emerged first, on 24 January. They were starving.

Garnet and Oldcorne held out until 27 January. They had been fed gruel or soup through a 'straw' passed between two chimneys. Their main problem had been that there was no toilet in the priesthole and they couldn't stand the smell any longer!

ANYONE FOR ORANGE JUICE?

Garnet was got. At last, the government had its hands on the man himself, the leader of the Jesuits, the real public enemy No. 1. To begin with he was treated gently. James himself interviewed him. Garnet was accused of having a relationship with Anne Vaux, his devoted Catholic follower who had hidden him on many occasions. This was untrue and unpleasant but not exactly serious.

The gentleness was a trick. Garnet was allowed enough freedom to smuggle letters out of the Tower of London to his supporters in London. Important bits were written in orange juice which makes an invisible ink until heated up. Child's play to Cecil's men. The letters were opened and read.

Fathers Garnet and Oldcorne were put in next door cells. A small opening meant they could talk to each

115

other without being overheard - or so it seemed. Actually government agents were hidden nearby and took notes of everything the two priests said to each other.

On 2 March 1606, Little John died, having been badly tortured and five days later, on 7 March, the kid gloves came off for Garnet. He was either tortured or threatened with torture. Next day he confessed to having known about the Plot before it took place. This was an offence called 'misprision of treason' because he hadn't warned the authorities. They now had more than enough 'evidence' to put him on trial, and trials, of course, were only for the 'guilty'.

A CHOP OFF THE OLD BLOCK

Ashley, Oldcorne and some others were executed in April. Father Garnet himself was executed in the churchyard of St. Paul's Cathedral, on 5 May 1606. A large crowd came to watch him die. They were no doubt curious to see what a top 'papist' looked like. However, when the time came to cut him down from the hangman's noose, the crowd took pity on him.

Someone shouted 'hold, hold' and those at the front pushed forward. They tugged at his legs. This helped him to die quickly. He was totally dead before the cutting up started.

You could even say he was lucky.

On the very same day, Father Gerard finally escaped from England, disguised as a servant in the party of some foreign envoys returning to the continent. Cecil had succeeded. The Plot was finally over - and so was the Jesuit plan for England.

THE BIRTH OF BONFIRE NIGHT

PLEASE TO REMEMBER

CLAMPDOWN

The execution of Father Garnet pretty well wrapped up the Gunpowder Plot. Various Catholic noblemen were locked up for a while and had to pay large fines, but mostly they were pretty comfortable. The Catholic Earl of Northumberland was allowed a study, a library, a drawing room and two dining rooms in his prison quarters in the Tower of London.

Even so, the whole thing was a disaster for Catholics. Protestants took advantage of the Plot to clamp down on them even harder than before.

No Catholic could carry a weapon except in self defence.

No Catholic could be an officer in the army or navy.

No Catholic could go to university.

No Catholic could stand for Parliament.

It wasn't until 1829 that Catholics were allowed back into Parliament, and even today it's against the law for a Catholic to be king or queen of England.

BONFIRE NIGHT

After the session which started on 5 November, Parliament met again on 21 January 1606 - while Garnet, Gerard and the others were still hiding in their priestholes. That was when the bill was passed making 5 November a day of public thanksgiving, the start of 'Bonfire Night' in other words. In fact, the act of Parliament was just a rubber stamp for what had already happened. Back on 5 November 1605, immediately after the plot was first discovered, bonfires had been lit all over London to celebrate. The mood in London had been so wild and angry that even Catholic ambassadors to London lit bonfires, just in case the Protestant crowd came and lit bonfires for them! The government allowed the bonfires so long as they were:

... without any danger of disorder.

GOOD FIRE, EH? WE SHOULD HAVE BURNED A PAPIST ON IT!

YEAH!

WE'LL MAKE A DUMMY OF GUY FAWKES FOR THE NEXT ONE!

YEAH!

AND THE ONE AFTER THAT!

FLAG DAY

Every year from then on, on top of our bonfires we place an effigy of Guy Fawkes, except of course we don't think of him as a real person who once plotted murder and suffered horribly for it. No one nowadays can possibly hate the real Guy Fawkes enough to want to burn him to death!

WHAT A GREAT GUY - EH? GOOD OR WHAT?

WELL - I HATE HIM!

WHY?

'COZ YOU'VE DRESSED HIM IN MY BEST SHIRT!

But it's easy enough to imagine the passions which allowed a group of men to plot murder. Easy to imagine because fanatical terrorists still plant bombs, and frightened governments still oppress minorities, thus helping to turn people into twisted terrorists. Many of us still wave our flags, flags of religion, race and nationality, even if (for most of us) our flags no longer say 'Catholic' or 'Protestant'.

It's best to remember, if anyone gets too heated about race, religion or politics, that those who wave their flags too hard will probably end up looking either sad, bad or ridiculous a few hundred years down the line. If we have to wave flags, the flag of tolerance is one of the few which doesn't seem to fade.

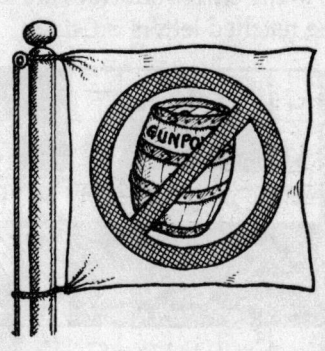

INTENSIVE VICAR FARM

(Pages 14/15)

Other things wrong:

1. One vicar has a wine goblet in his pocket.
2. Another vicar has a crucifix.
3. There's a woman!
4. There's a Spitfire in the sky.
5. The school has TV aerials.

PLOT CROSS FUN

(Page 71)

1. The secret message read: *The penalty for writing in this book is to be hung drawn and quartered!*

2. Answers to the crossword clues are shown below. The name in the hatched letters is: *Catesby*

Jesuit Jobsearch

(Page 81)

Remember, you've got to make sure that you don't stand out in a crowd - yet you've got to be brave, clever and able to communicate well.

	A	B	C	Comments
1. Height	0	1	3	Being short would be good for hiding in priestholes!
2. Conversation	1	3	0	Keeping secrets is one of a priest's main jobs.
3. Intelligence	3	1	0	Clever yes - but not too clever for your own good!
4. Courage	3	1	0	With the death penalty for being caught, are you up to it?
5. Appearance	0	3	1	But being scruffy may help you to blend into a crowd!
6. Languages	3	1	0	You may need to speak French, German, Spanish, English - and Latin.

Scores

18	Top class Jesuit.
13-16	Not too bad.
7-12	You might last a few weeks.
1-6	Stay in your priesthole!
0	You're for the chop.

HAH!

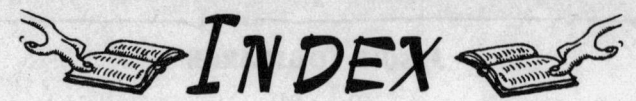
INDEX

WHAT NEXT?

If you can get to London, or you live there already, why not visit the torture chambers of the Tower of London where Guy and his friends were questioned? It's a pretty morbid thing to do, but the reality of those dismal rooms brings home the horror of what they went through like nothing else.

The Great Hall at Westminster where the trial took place is also worth a look. It's one of the most complete medieval buildings in Britain and the scene of many other major historical events, such as the trial of Charles I. As background, take a look at a complete version of the Gunpowder Plot trial in the original language at:

http://www.armitstead.com/gunpowder/trial.html

Also, the website of the 'Centre for Fawkesian Pursuits' is worth a visit at:

http://www.bcpl.lib.md.us/cbladey/guy/html/main.html

ABOUT THE AUTHOR

Bob Fowke is a popular author of children's information books. Writing under various pen names and with various friends and colleagues, he has created many unusual and entertaining works on all manner of subjects.

There's always more to his books than meets the eye - look at all the entries in the index of this one!

What They Don't Tell You About ...

ORDER FORM

0 340 70921 9	ANGLO SAXONS	£3.99
0 340 71330 5	ART	£3.99
0 340 85183 X	THE BLITZ	£4.99
0 340 78806 2	CHARLES I AND THE CIVIL WAR	£3.99
0 340 78807 0	THE COLD WAR	£3.99
0 340 65613 1	ELIZABETH I	£3.99
0 340 63621 1	HENRY VIII	£3.99
0 340 69349 5	LIVING THINGS	£3.99
0 340 73611 9	OLYMPICS	£3.99
0 340 71329 1	PLANET EARTH	£3.99
0 340 63622 X	QUEEN VICTORIA	£3.99
0 340 70922 7	ROMANS	£3.99
0 340 67093 2	SHAKESPEARE	£3.99
0 340 68995 1	STORY OF MUSIC	£3.99
0 340 69350 9	STORY OF SCIENCE	£3.99
0 340 78805 4	WORLD WAR I	£3.99
0 340 68612 X	WORLD WAR II	£3.99

All Hodder Children's books are available at your local bookshop or newsagent, or can be ordered direct from the publisher. Just write to the address below. Prices and availability subject to change without notice.

Hodder Children's Books, Cash Sales Department, Bookpoint, 130 Milton Park, Abingdon, Oxon, OX14 4SB, UK.
Email address: orders@bookpoint.co.uk

Please enclose a cheque or postal order made payable to Bookpoint Ltd to the value of the cover price and allow the following for postage and packing:
UK & BFPO - £1.00 for the first book, 50p for the second book, and 30p for each additional book ordered, up to a maximum charge of £3.00. OVERSEAS & EIRE - £2.00 for the first book, £1.00 for the second book, and 50p for each additional book.

If you have a credit card you may order by telephone - (01235) 400414 (lines open 9am-6pm, Monday to Saturday; 24 hour message answering service). Alternatively you can send a fax on 01235 400454.